This
SIDE UP!

A Simple Guide To Your
Successful Relocation

By Lauren Herring, CEO of IMPACT Group

Foreword by Shellye Archambeau, CEO of MetricStream

www.ThisSideUpGuide.com

This Side Up: A Simple Guide to Your Successful Relocation

Lauren Herring

Print ISBN: 978-1-48357-232-1

eBook ISBN: 978-1-48357-233-8

Contents

8. Job Hunting

9. Settling In

Conclusion

Foreword

By Shellye Archambeau, CEO of MetricStream

If I were writing my life story, I'd probably title it "I've Been Moved."

Throughout my life, I have lived and worked in seventeen different places—first with my parents, then with my husband, and eventually with our two children. Stressful? It can be. Worth it? Completely. I would do it all again in a heartbeat.

Some of the best experiences we've had, as a family, have resulted from taking the risk and moving to new areas, new regions, and new countries. Learning about people from the perspective of culture, geography, and language has greatly added to the quality and richness of our lives, when I look back.

Of course it hasn't been easy. Every relocation means leaving behind friends and organizations we've come to love. Saying goodbye never feels great. And there is always anxiety about the future, always sacrifice, always difficult decisions.

Still, for us, relocation has always been a choice to move forward, toward the future we are building. For my daughter and son, relocation has given them an immense collection of life skills and unique cultural perspectives that can only be gained through new experiences. As for my husband and myself, the excitement of building something special, and the hard work of going through all these life changes together, has strengthened our partnership and taught us what family truly means to us.

Personally, I've been a planner since I was very young. Even in high school, I knew I wanted to run a company one day. How would I get there? I crafted a strategy that led me to the Wharton School of Business, with summers spent interning at IBM. It was there I met the man who would become my husband, and we decided to move forward together into the next phase of our lives.

And so, as a college graduate in my twenties, I found myself watching the tides of my life change: I was preparing to move to Dallas, get married, begin my career, and start a family too—oh yes, all that at once. I was a bundle of nerves: excited, scared, totally in love, and overwhelmingly anxious about what was to come.

When we arrived in Dallas, I told my husband I didn't want to live out of boxes any longer than necessary. "Let's give ourselves a time limit to move in," I told him—always planning. We decided on a bold strategy: after one month, we were going to throw a party at our new house. We invited everyone we ran into: neighbors, acquaintances, the handyman. And sure enough, a month after the move, our house was relatively put together and we were surrounded by smiling faces. It actually felt a little bit like a home.

With as many times as we've moved since, I think we've had just about every relocation-related experience imaginable. From navigating the streets of Tokyo as an expat family, to my commuting from California to Dallas while my daughter finished high school, we've really done it all. Every relocation has been different, because we are different people moving to a different place. And yet, every relocation has been part of the plan, and it has always benefited us to take the risk and make the move.

Fast forward to the early 2010s, at a meeting of the Committee of 200 (an organization for leading female entrepreneurs and executives). A charismatic young executive, Lauren Herring, spoke about her role with IMPACT Group, and the relocation support services it provides. Afterward, I introduced myself and told Lauren my own story, with its seventeen different locations and chapters. "I really understand the value of what you do," I said. What I was soon to discover, however, is that Lauren's extraordinary dedication to her work makes IMPACT Group even stronger, and its work even more valuable.

Lauren is energetic and passionate about what she does. She treats the objective of her company—helping others succeed through transitions—as her personal mission. It's inspiring to see how much of herself she gives to this cause, and in the years since our first meeting, I've come to appreciate her not just as a professional acquaintance, but as a friend.

Throughout my seventeen different lives, I've experienced varying levels of relocation support. Some moves have been completely DIY, lifting each box ourselves. Other times, we've had help at every step. Several times, we've received some financial help to make the move affordable, but have had to take care of all the details on our own.

After all this time, I can say with great certainty that moving is one of the most stressful things you can do. Relocation means that, all of a sudden, you've got a long list of things that have to get done in a short period of time. It means facing seemingly uncountable unknowns and endless decisions. It's exhausting as much as it is exciting—and any help you can get makes a real difference.

IMPACT Group provides each family with a relocation coach to help organize all the tasks, smooth the path, and give expert guidance along the way. It's an extremely beneficial model, and I believe Lauren and her organization are fully committed to making sure it works for the people who need it most. However, IMPACT Group can't work with everyone; even for their clients, coaches can't be there for every single conversation and daily decision. That's where this book comes in.

My family has moving down to a science, but that doesn't mean we do it the same way each time. There's a big difference between moving within the same state, for example, as opposed to moving halfway across the world. Each time, there are decisions to be made; possessions and expectations to be managed; and always, always important family conversations about how we want to approach this next stage in our life plan—as a team, and with respect to everyone's needs and wishes.

I told you I'm a planner, and I believe planning and strategy, paired with compassion and relationships, have gotten me just about everywhere I wanted to be in life. I have complete certainty that, with a solid plan, you too will succeed at getting wherever you're going. The advice in this book is based on decades of experience and thousands of relocation stories; it is truly invaluable for the process you're entering into with your upcoming move.

Just to make sure you've got all the information you need, I've added a few tips from my own life into each chapter. I hope they help, or at least entertain, as you make your own decisions, craft your plans, and look forward to the future you are building now.

Best of luck with your relocation!

Introduction

I was born and raised in St. Louis, Missouri, and lived there until college. A few years after graduation, when I returned to my hometown, I was shocked. St. Louis felt like a brand-new city, and I was a new person in it. I had to find new friends, new activities, a new way of living. It took a good year before I felt settled in to this place where I had spent most of my life.

This is the power of relocation: it truly changes everything when you move. And it's funny that, even as someone whose family is all employed in the relocation industry, I could not understand this until it happened to me.

This concept—that relocation is a life-shaking event and one that's difficult to understand—is the driving idea behind my company, IMPACT Group. As a girl, my mother and IMPACT Group's founder, Laura Herring, moved with her family from New Jersey to Missouri, and then to Tennessee. This final relocation marked the end of her idyllic childhood in many ways. She never forgot the stress and strain of that move, and later, as a psychologist, she observed that relocation had similar effects on many of her clients. This is what drove her to approach corporations and tell them that there is a better way—that with the right support and guidance, relocation can be a more positive experience.

IMPACT Group was created to help, and I'm proud to say that's what we have done. If you get a chance, read my mother's memoir, *No Fear Allowed: A Story of Guts, Perseverance, & Making an IMPACT.* Since she founded the company in 1988, we've helped over 100,000 families adapt to new locations as well as find jobs. We've been rated #1 in the industry year after year[1].

Most people probably don't ever think about such a thing as a "relocation industry," yet the average American moves eleven times in his or her life. Every move is different, and every move is stressful. There are countless hidden pitfalls, surprises—and never enough time, it seems.

Over the decades as we've supported people through this process, we've noticed something else: the process of relocation brings up the same emotions as the stages of grief. Moving truly is like grieving, for many, as you say goodbye to a place, a community, and people you love. Denial, anger, bargaining, and acceptance are really the phases of letting go.

The emotional roller coaster of this process can surprise you: from the initial high of excitement and hope for the future, things can easily plunge into loneliness or worry. Eventually, however, the new place does become your home, and happiness returns. In fact, we believe that relocating can bring all sorts of new joys and experiences. Our job is to help people get there as quickly and smoothly as possible.

At IMPACT Group, we accomplish this by assigning each family a relocation "coach" to help them sort through all the information, talk through the issues, make decisions, and stay organized. This book is designed to fulfill a similar role in your move. Moving isn't rocket science, but it can be complicated, frustrating, and overwhelming at times. My goal with this book is to provide you with simple, expert advice from people who have "been there and done that" as it relates to moving. Perhaps even think of it as sitting at the coffee shop with a friend you trust who can provide you guidance from all her personal experiences. We've filled these pages with the best and most valuable information gleaned from years of experience and thousands of stories. Take these ideas and make them your own! In

---

1 Source: Trippel Relocation Managers Surveys, Trippel Survey and Research LLC (http://trippelsurvey.com/relocation-managers-surveys.html)

fact, as you read this book, I encourage you to visit the book's webpage, www.ThisSideUpGuide.com, as we have also made the worksheets and exercises available to you there as well.

I'm proud of what all the dedicated people at IMPACT Group, including my parents, have accomplished, and I'm so grateful to be a part of it. And now, it is my pleasure to share our collected experience and wisdom with you.

Happy moving!

Lauren Herring

CEO, IMPACT Group

PART ONE

Your Relocation Roadmap

1. Do This First

The one decision to make before anything else

So, you're moving.

From this moment, a long road stretches ahead of you. You will travel across great distances, overcome countless obstacles, navigate new territories…and at the end of it all, you will arrive in your new home, safe and sound and ready to face the future.

For some people reading this book, you may have a year or more to complete your relocation. For others, it might be only a few months (or even weeks). Some have families to think of; others will move solo. Some people have support from their employers, and the funds to hire service providers; others will pack and carry each box. Yet, despite the wide variety of possible experiences, nearly everyone facing a relocation goes through the same emotions.

Are you excited? Apprehensive? Perhaps you are frustrated or even a little angry. New emotions rise up at every turn, with every new thought—*What about the kids' school year? How will I make new friends? What's going to happen with selling our house?*—until you may become completely overwhelmed.

Feeling overwhelmed is completely normal: whether you're relocating for the first time or the fifth, there are a lot of decisions to be made very quickly. How will you strategize for a successful relocation, making

everything go smoothly while maintaining your household's collective sanity?

That's where this book comes in. In these pages, you'll find the information you need to make your big move a successful one. The people contributing to this book have experience moving personally, as well as decades of experience guiding thousands of people through their own relocations. You can trust that the information here is solid, trustworthy, and reliable. Think of this book as your personal relocation guide, here to advise you every step of the way.

Attitude + action = outcome

Karen has relocated her family six times over the years. When her son was a teenager, the family needed to move again. Karen's son lived for his baseball team, and didn't want to leave his friends and teammates. So she called the baseball coach at a school in the new location, and told him the situation.

"I get it," the coach said. "My family moved when I was in high school, too." He gave Karen the names of some local teams, and information on the school sports programs.

After the move, Karen's son tried out for a good team and made the cut. Not only did his new teammates become close friends, but they eventually went on to play in a national-level competition.

The One Decision You Should Make Today

When it comes to making a lot of decisions in a short period of time, clear intention cuts right through emotion. That is to say: **it's best to set your** priorities *before you do anything else*. Once you know what you want—when your top priority is clear—you can begin to see the path ahead. This will inform every decision you make in this early stage of the relocation process, and it will help all those future decisions make more sense.

Our experts work with people and families of all types. Here are a few of the common situations we've seen people overcome (and even enjoy) during the relocation process:

- Jim took a new job and had to report to work right away. He moved into temporary housing in the new city, while Maria stayed behind so their daughters could finish the school year. During the summer break, the family reunited in a new home.

- Amy found work right away, but Eric needed more time to acquire a teaching license and find a position. In the meantime, they made do on a single income.

- Michael was transferred, but Denise didn't want to leave the city where she had finally put down roots. With three years left before his retirement, the couple decided to live separately: Denise stayed in their home while Michael rented an apartment and commuted home once a month. Three years later, he moved back.

- Straight out of grad school, Sara found an amazing opportunity in her field of study—in Japan. Saying goodbye to her friends and family, she embarked on a new career and life, not sure if her path would someday bring her back home.

Whatever you're going through, you are not the first to face this major life change. Knowing that you're not alone, and that support and resources are available, you now must choose: how will you make this relocation a happy one?

Your first decision, therefore, is to adopt a positive attitude. Not everyone reading this book will want to take that first step; but those who do will have vastly better experiences moving into a new life situation.

In our decades of guiding thousands of relocations each year, we consistently see that the people who keep a positive outlook also have a better experience.

For some, having a positive attitude will be easy. Perhaps you're excited about moving to a place you've always wanted to go, or you're eager to follow a fantastic career opportunity. Maybe you've got a once-in-a-lifetime chance to live in a new country for a few years. If this is you, congratulations! Keep that positive outlook.

If you're having trouble seeing the silver lining, take a few minutes and try to visualize your life in the new location. **What are some positive changes you can make, now that you know you're moving? Perhaps you'll find a home with a better yard, or a neighborhood with great character. Maybe you'll find a school, church, or club that really suits your values. What positive opportunities can you envision?**

When you've got ideas in mind for how your new life looks, don't be shy: turn those ideas into your new goals! The biggest positive aspect of relocation, after all, is the possibility of reinventing and improving various facets of your lifestyle.

Whether you are 25 or 55, updating your personal vision of who and what you want to be is critical to feeling you are in control of YOU. So take a few minutes now to create that vision, and then make it your reality.

Home, a world away

When Andrew and family found out he was being transferred to Oslo, they were simultaneously excited and scared. Andrew and his wife decided the best course of action would be to find other people who had moved to Norway, and ask them what to expect. The more they learned, the more confident they felt—having real expectations helped them dispel their fears and even made them more excited. In the process, they found an expats' group full of people who would welcome them and help them feel at home once they arrived.

Goal Setting and Priorities

Now that you've envisioned your new life, it's time to let that vision guide the many, *many* choices and actions ahead. At the end of this chapter, you'll find a worksheet that will help you set some important priorities.

In our experience, relocation needs can be broken out into five categories:

1. Relationships

2. Lifestyle

3. Location

4. Finance & Legal

5. Careers

Each of these categories gives you plenty to consider. For example, relationships: Do you want to stay close to family members if possible? Would you like it to be relatively easy and affordable to visit them? Are there friends you'd like to live near? How about making friends in your new location? The Setting Priorities worksheet at the end of this chapter will help you assign a priority to each of these ideas.

Once you gain clarity on what is truly important, your decisions will become easier. Instead of going back and forth over every choice, you can simply ask yourself: *Does this get me closer to my goal? Is this going to help me keep my priorities straight? How will my choice help me create the life I've been envisioning?*

As you fill out this worksheet, try to be completely honest about what matters in your day-to-day life. What will make everything work smoothly? What would be nice, but might not make much difference? Refer back to that vision of your future, and don't be afraid to go for what you really want. If you are married or in a partnership, we highly recommend that you involve your partner in this process. There is no better time to make sure you're both on the same page, both in agreement about what you want, and both ready to move forward!

Remember, the most important decision you have to make will set the tone for this transition. This is especially important when you're moving with children. We recommend choosing to be positive and go after the things you really want; with this positive attitude, you'll be surprised how much you can accomplish.

In the next chapter, we'll guide you through some tough conversations as you break the news to family and friends, and we'll help you find strategies to involve the whole family in your relocation planning—including making those tough choices about schools and activities.

Before you skip ahead, take the time to complete the Setting Priorities worksheet. Over decades of assisting people with their relocations, we have found this to be a highly valuable part of the process. So give yourself a little time, take a deep breath, and start to envision your future!

You know yourself best!

When Matt and Kim moved to San Francisco, their friends advised them to look at outlying areas, where they could find a larger home at a lower price. However, Matt knew that would mean at least two hours' commute time each day—time he'd rather spend at home. Instead, they took a smaller place in the city, knowing that the size of their house was less important to them than the chance to enjoy more free time.

Shellye's Tip: Don't let stress take over!

Staying positive during a relocation is easier if you've got a good strategy for managing your stress. Personally, I work out in the mornings—it's a simple thing that helps me feel healthy and in control, while helping with stress. I also work off of to-do lists: it feels good to write things down, and then mark them as completed.

Whatever your own techniques are for day-to-day happiness, I think it's crucial to have diversity in your life. For example, in addition to my professional life, it's important to me to be involved in my community, and engaged with my family (including extended family). Your choices may be different, but it's wise to wear more than one hat. Not least because, if things are difficult in one area of your life, you've still got the others!

Smart Moves

Decide to Have a Positive Attitude.

You can't always control what happens, but you can control your reaction. You have the power to choose whether you want this process to be something you just "get through," or something you approach proactively. Don't fake happiness or deny your emotions—simply choose to make the very best out of the opportunities ahead.

Set Your Priorities.

When you know what you want, you have the power to go get it. And when your household all agrees on (or at least understands) what is important to each other, you can support each other more effectively. Take the time to really gain clarity on what is most important to you, and let your priorities guide all the decisions to come.

Worksheet: Setting Priorities

Use this worksheet to clarify what is truly important to you. The priorities you set here will guide your future decisions as you continue with your relocation.

Relationships

The people we love play a vital role in our happiness and wellbeing. What will help you stay close to those who are most important to you? Remember, thanks to technology, you don't always need to live near someone to feel close.

How important are the following factors in your transition and integration into the new community?

Rank each line from 1 to 7, with 1 being most important.

___ Maintaining close relationships with family members who are not moving with you

___ Being close to current friends

___ Travel time and expense for visits with family and friends

___ Family commitments and events

___ Meeting new friends

___ Relocating with your partner and/or nuclear family

___ Other: _____

Lifestyle

Your lifestyle is all the choices you and your family make from day to day. This includes education, activities, recreation, health, and more. In order to be happy in your new life, you should decide which activities you cherish, which pastimes you'll pursue, and how you plan to take care of yourself.

Which of these lifestyle factors are relevant to you? It could be all of them, or just a few.

Check all the relevant boxes, then answer the questions in those categories.

☐   Health & Wellness

☐   Resources for Children

☐   Education (Primary and Secondary)

☐   Higher Education

☐   Eldercare

☐   Pets

☐   Spiritual Life

☐   Recreation & Community Involvement

☐   Arts & Entertainment

Health & Wellness

Your health and wellness needs are vital to your happiness. These may have changed since you last moved, or they may change in the future; take the long view as you consider this category.

How important are the following factors in your transition and acclimation?

Rank each line from 1 to 6, with 1 being most important.

__ Easy access to healthcare

__ Options and quality of healthcare providers

__ Fitness centers or wellness programs

__ Critical or chronic health concerns

__ Special needs services and care

__ Other: _____

Resources for Children

Finding the right caregivers, lessons, and activities for children can help the entire family to acclimate more quickly.

How important are the following factors in your transition and acclimation?

Rank each line from 1 to 5, with 1 being most important.

__ Daycare options

__ Preschool quality and options

__ Babysitters

__ Children's lessons and activities

__ Other: _____

Education

Finding the right school(s) is a priority for many families. Relocating gives you the opportunity to consider your needs and preferences for education. What do you want to look into?

How important are the following factors in your transition and acclimation?

Rank each line from 1 to 6, with 1 being most important.

__ Public education quality and options

__ Private education quality and options

__ Special education quality and options

__ Access to specialized courses of study

__ Extracurricular activities

__ Other: _____

Higher Education

If college or an advanced degree is in the cards for anyone in the family, consider the resources needed to pursue those educational goals, as well as any plans already in place.

How important are the following factors in your transition and acclimation?

Rank each line from 1 to 4, with 1 being most important.

__ Suitability of colleges, universities, and trade schools in the region

__ Credit transfer policy of potential institutions

__ Tuition and costs for residents and non-residents

__ Other: _____

Eldercare

As with healthcare, it's wise to look into the future as you evaluate your needs for eldercare. What will your needs be in a few years? How will your relocation affect any existing needs?

How important are the following factors in your transition and acclimation?

Rank each line from 1 to 6, with 1 being most important.

__ Retirement communities

__ Assisted living options

__ Skilled nursing homes

__ In-home care or assistance

__ Community resources and activities

__ Other: _____

Pets

Our faithful friends have needs of their own. If you have a pet, consider what will make it easier for you to care for it in the new location.

How important are the following factors in your transition and acclimation?

Rank each line from 1 to 4, with 1 being most important.

__ Veterinarian care and access

__ Local regulations for vaccinations, registration, quarantine, breeds, etc.

__ Additional resources such as boarding, parks, etc.

__ Other: _____

Spiritual Life

In times of transition, spirituality can help us feel grounded and connected; churches and other organizations can also be places to make new friends. What would you like to look into?

How important are the following factors in your transition and acclimation?

Rank each line from 1 to 4, with 1 being most important.

__ Places of worship that might be comparable to your previous experience

__ Access to a spiritual community

__ Spiritual diversity of the new community

__ Other: _____

Recreation & Community Involvement

Not only are sports, volunteering, and other activities good ways to fill your life, but they are also opportunities to make friends. What activities would you like to engage in?

How important are the following factors in your transition and acclimation?

Rank each line from 1 to 5, with 1 being most important.

__ Regional sports community, including professional or college games to attend

__ Local sports leagues, adult recreational leagues, or group activities

__ Access to volunteer opportunities

___ Resources for other hobbies & interests (music, arts, cooking, etc.)

___ Other: _____

Arts & Entertainment

Do you love discovering new restaurants? Enjoy concerts in the park or local theater? Consider the entertainment options that will add variety to your life.

How important are the following factors in your transition and acclimation?

Rank each line from 1 to 6, with 1 being most important.

___ Theater and performing arts

___ Concerts and music venues

___ Options and quality for dining out

___ Social events and nightlife

___ Festivals and community events

___ Other: _____

Location

In most areas, you will have many neighborhoods and communities to choose from. A community's options for housing, culture, environment, and transportation will all affect your life in many ways. Weigh each of these factors as you answer the following questions.

Housing

No matter what, you'll need housing in the new location. As you consider your options, think about whether your needs have changed since your last move, or whether they could change soon.

How important are the following factors in your transition and acclimation?

Rank each line from 1 to 4, with 1 being most important.

__ Availability and options for temporary housing

__ Rental housing availability and options

__ Housing market: availability, cost, and features of homes for sale

__ Other: _____

Culture

Whether you will be moving to a new country or just to another region, your new community can have its own culture, customs, demographics, even languages. What is important for you to feel at home in your new home?

How important are the following factors in your transition and acclimation?

Rank each line from 1 to 7, with 1 being most important.

__ Diversity and demographics of a new community

__ Local languages spoken

__ Options and types of cuisine and markets

__ Expatriate organizations and resources

___ Social and/or religious communities

___ Business and political customs

___ Other: _____

Environment

The world begins at your doorstep; settling into the right environment can be vital to wellbeing and adjustment. What neighborhood factors are important for your transition?

How important are the following factors in your transition and acclimation?

Rank each line from 1 to 6, with 1 being most important.

___ Crime rates and safety concerns

___ Environmental conditions including weather, climate, and air quality

___ Access to parks and open spaces

___ Aesthetics such as architectural styles and neighborhood layout

___ Urban vs. rural setting

___ Other: _____

Transportation

Getting around in a new community may not work the way it used to. Evaluate your commuting and transportation options and how they will affect your transition.

How important are the following factors in your transition and acclimation?

Rank each line from 1 to 5, with 1 being most important.

___ Traffic and daily commute times

___ Public transportation options

___ Vehicle insurance costs and options

___ Long-distance travel options

___ Other: _____

Finance & Legal

With relocation come changes to your financial situation and, in some cases, to your legal status. Weigh each of these factors carefully so you can take initiative on any necessary actions, sooner than later.

Finance

Changes in your financial situation and the cost of living in the new community can leave you with some budget adjustments to make. What information should you prepare ahead of time to make the transition easier?

How important are the following factors in your transition and acclimation?

Rank each line from 1 to 7, with 1 being most important.

___ Total income compared to cost of living

___ Sale and value of your home and/or property

___ Purchase or rental costs in the new area

___ Credit scores and loan availability

___ Mortgage availability and rates

___ Banking options

___ Other: _____

Legal

If you have existing, pending, or upcoming legal matters, it is crucial to take early action. What resources will you need as you move to a new location?

How important are the following factors in your transition and acclimation?

Rank each line from 1 to 7, with 1 being most important.

___ Domestic partnership and/or common law

___ Immigration eligibility for your family

___ Your family's eligibility for work authorizations

___ Child custody arrangements

___ Pending litigation

___ Military commitments

___ Other: _____

Careers

Whether you're relocating for a job opportunity or will be seeking a job in the new location, your career is a central element of your new life.

Check the box or boxes that apply to you, then answer the questions under the corresponding category.

☐ I have employment in the new location

☐ I will be seeking employment in the new location

I have employment in the new location:

Congratulations! Your new job will set you off on the right foot. Nonetheless, you may have questions still to be answered, including your future career plans.

How important are the following factors in your transition and acclimation?

Rank each line from 1 to 8, with 1 being most important.

__ Career development and future opportunities for advancement

__ Opportunities for training and mentorship

__ Value of compensation and benefits package in the new location

__ Employer reputation and company culture

__ Opportunity and support for work/life balance

__ Likelihood of long-term employment

__ Availability of comparable jobs in the area

__ Other: _____

I will be seeking employment in the new location:

Relocation comes with both opportunities and challenges. Some use a move as a chance to seek out new careers, entrepreneurial ventures, or other professional moves. Others might prefer to stay on their existing career track, but need additional training or licensing.

How important are the following factors in your transition and acclimation?

Rank each line from 1 to 12, with 1 being most important.

__ Availability of comparable or desired jobs in your field

__ Compensation rates and/or income potential

__ Certification or licensure requirements

__ Job search strategy, tools, and resources

__ Updated resume and/or professional profile

__ Local hiring customs and negotiating tactics

__ Relocation of existing business

__ Startup of a new business

__ Networking opportunities and professional associations

__ Exploration of (or transition to) a new field of employment

__ Career coaching or mentorship

__ Other: _____

Your Top Priorities

Look at the top one or two priorities you chose for each section. If an item is critical to the success of your move, write it in the space below. These are your top priorities! Keep them in mind when you make important decisions about your relocation.

2. Family Meeting

Including the whole team in relocation planning

The family that plans together, moves together—give or take a few in-between stages. By now, you may have realized that relocation isn't as simple as packing up and driving into the sunset. If you have kids, you might be thinking about their school year, their sports, and their friends. Family members and friends might not be thrilled to see you leave.

As excited as you may be about your move, it can be tough to figure out the right way to break the news to loved ones. It might be tempting to just not tell them—to simply keep your move under wraps for now.

"I'll tell them in a couple of weeks, once I've got a plan," you might be thinking. Our relocation experts hear this all the time—and we'd like to advise you against keeping your move a secret, even for a little while.

Your family is the greatest team you'll have in life. When a family works together toward a shared goal, the results can be wonderful. However, a family is made up of individual people, each of whom have their own personalities, priorities, and expectations. Want to get everyone on the team? You'll need to give them enough time to get excited about the idea, and an opportunity to set their own priorities. This goes for your spouse of twenty years just as much as your five-year-old: when big changes are coming, we all want to be prepared.

So how *do* you tell them? That's what this chapter is all about. We'll discuss the various emotions members of your family might be feeling; give you expert advice for how to include everyone; and provide some tools to plan together as a team.

It's all about open communication, honesty, and respect. Are you ready to coach your family team to a victorious move?

What can you both agree on?

Cam and Gina moved from their hometown in Illinois to Boston, leaving behind their families and lifelong friends—but they always knew it would be temporary. However, three years later when Cam was transferred back home, Gina realized she didn't want to go. She had grown to love their new city, and their daughter was happy in school.

The couple knew their top priority was to have a happy life together, no matter what. So Cam negotiated a later start date at the new position, giving them a few more months' time. Their daughter was able to finish the year at her school, and Gina had enough time to say goodbye. They were able to relocate without rushing the process or splitting up and moving separately. It wasn't a perfect solution, but they fulfilled their top priority of keeping the family together.

Talking To Your Partner

In the previous chapter, we advised you to work with your partner to set the big priorities that will guide your relocation decisions. But what if you're not sure how to start the conversation?

If this move wasn't a mutual decision (for example, if you're being transferred), then it's important to talk it out honestly. **Remember: nobody can**

force you to move. It's crucial that this decision takes into account your priorities as a couple, and as individuals.

Here's an example of a situation our relocation experts often see: Rebecca is offered a promotion in a new city. If she says no, she loses the opportunity. However, her husband Josh has built a successful psychology practice with clients who depend on him; if he leaves, he'll have to start again from scratch.

There are always more options than you might imagine. Rebecca could reject the job and look for a comparable position in their current city. Or, Josh could move right away, and continue to counsel his clients remotely. Rebecca could even take the new job and live in temporary housing while Josh closes down his practice and sets up a new one; then they could move into a more permanent home together.

In order to truly know what's best for both of you, you'll have to hash it out. If possible, give your partner a little time to think about it. Ask him or her to set individual priorities. Then sit down, talk through your feelings, and compare your goals.

Listen for the Win-Win Solution

Whether it's a mutual decision, or fate is forcing your hand; whether you're both excited about the opportunity, or there's some tension in the mix; there is almost always a way to make everyone happy. Quite often, the way to find it is through listening to your partner.

There are no rules governing what you have to do; as partners, you make the rules. Therefore, consider all your options. What conditions, and how much time, do you and your partner need to successfully relocate and settle into a new place? How can you create a plan that suits both your needs and timelines?

Negotiation can be tricky, but if you both commit to finding a solution that works, you might be surprised at how easily one comes. Our relocation experts see this all the time: when both partners are working toward a positive outcome, it nearly always works out well.

Again, the key is to keep a positive attitude. As adults, you can both evaluate the situation proactively, and make wise decisions for your future. You can also look at some of the benefits that this move could bring: whether moving to a better climate, or a better neighborhood; finally getting a house with a pool; or reducing your commute. What are the positives, and how can they help this relocation become one of the best moves you can make?

Emotions change as kids grow up

Jenny's daughter was five when they moved. To make the process a positive one, Jenny and Steve involved her in everything: from house hunting to packing. It wasn't always easy; there were breakdowns. "You have to remember what is appropriate for a child's age," Jenny says. "At five, your emotions only last ten minutes. So she was distraught for ten minutes, and then it passed." By not avoiding her daughter's emotions and allowing her to express them, Jenny also allowed them to pass.

Marlie's daughter, on the other hand, was in high school and heavily involved in her cheer squad. When it came time to move, she took the news badly—even going behind her parents' backs to find friends she could stay with instead of moving. Rather than simply putting her foot down, Marlie recognized her daughter's fears. She called the cheer team coach in the new area and asked for some information and introductions. The day the family arrived in their new location, a member of the cheer team was waiting to pick her daughter up and take her to a meet-and-greet. In the end, she made new friends and fit in quickly with the new team.

Talking To Your Child(ren)

Relocation can be stressful and overwhelming for adults, but ultimately we know we're grownups and can handle whatever life throws at us. We don't always feel the same about our kids' ability to adapt to big changes. Families with children often go through much more emotional upheaval in the face of a move, and much of it is out of a desire to protect kids' hearts and minds from trauma.

What if moving didn't need to be traumatic? There are strategies to guide your children through this process quite happily—and one of the keys is to introduce the idea early on.

Our relocation experts work with families every day who come up with clever ways to keep the kids involved in the process. In fact, although the big decision is made by the grownups, letting the young ones help with smaller choices gives them more control over their fate, and helps them get excited about what's ahead.

Keeping everyone's priorities in mind

Carla and Jimmy's son David, an adult with autism, was very happy with his home and his work at a local community organization. When it came time to relocate, the couple determined that they would not move until they could be sure David would adjust to the new life.

They researched a vocational center in the new community, and found information on new job opportunities. This made David comfortable enough to say that he could probably settle in. When they told him the new house could be near the beach, that was enough to get David excited that his new life could be even better than the current one. The family was able to relocate successfully, and David immediately began a comfortable new routine.

Breaking the News

Be honest with your children, and maintain a positive attitude as you tell them about your reasons for moving. Kids take their emotional cues from their parents, and your subtle signals will help them share a positive outlook. At the same time, allow them to express whatever thoughts and feelings arise. Throughout the moving process, you should always listen and seek to understand, rather than telling your young ones not to worry or be sad.

Here are some things to keep in mind as you talk to your kids:

1. Be honest. Don't sugarcoat what will happen, or exaggerate the positive aspects; allow your children to process the information in their own way.

2. Provide a timeline. Give kids an idea of what will happen and when, so they can understand how it fits into their school year and other plans.

3. Give detail on what will happen. Talk about what is involved in finding a new home, selling your old one, finding work in the new location, and so on. Help your kids to feel involved and up to speed on what is happening, and continue updating them throughout the process.

4. Ask for feedback. While kids may not have a say in whether you move, they can have opinions on what kind of house and yard they would like, what sorts of activities they want to get involved in, even how to pack and sort their belongings. Find age-appropriate ways for kids to get excited about the possibilities while retaining a sense of control.

5. Allow and acknowledge a full range of emotions. You can't tell another person how to feel; when you try, it may make them feel worse. Whatever your kids are feeling, make an effort to listen to them and react appropriately—instead of telling them "don't worry, it'll be fine."

After this conversation, your first step is to give kids a timeline they can work with. One idea is to get a wall calendar—or use the timeline included in this chapter—and add specific events and tasks to specific dates, so your kids know what to look forward to. Your timeline might include things like going on house-hunting trips in the new town; researching new schools; packing and organizing; throwing a goodbye party; even scheduling future dates for visits with friends after your move. You can also make use of the timeline at the end of this chapter to help kids keep track of progress without getting overwhelmed in detail.

With older children and teenagers, give them as much information as possible to help them understand your decision. Younger children might be overwhelmed with too many abstract ideas, so keep it simple and concrete.

We've created an additional resource at RelocatingKids.com that can help everyone in your family prepare for this transition. Visit it now, and often throughout the process.

Shepherding the Emotional Journey

For young people going through a big life change without the ability to say "no," the adaptation process can look a lot like a grieving process. They will go through various emotional stages, and as a parent, the best thing you can do is to be attentive, and listen.

In some ways, this will depend on the age of your child, not to mention his or her personality. Older children and teenagers, particularly those with strong social connections, may be so strongly opposed to moving that you'll end up letting them finish the school year, rather than ripping them from their friendships. Younger kids, on the other hand, might simply be scared of the unknown—or they might be completely comfortable with whatever Mom and Dad think is best. Watch for signs of emotional upheaval, such as withdrawal or acting out. It may help to watch the Disney/Pixar film *Inside Out*—a story about a young girl adjusting to life in a new city—as a family!

Again, **it's crucial that you allow children and teenagers to express themselves emotionally. This may be the biggest life change they've experienced so far, and it is beyond their control in many ways. If they are having trouble, ask them to share more about how they feel. Most of the time, they simply need somebody to listen to them.** Often, you'll be able to do something to make them feel more in control.

We've included a worksheet at the end of this chapter, which can help each member of the family share his or her emotions. Try working through this exercise together, and see what results!

Remember, if you truly believe this is a good decision for your family, and if you've resolved to have a positive attitude, your excitement will be infectious. In the end, that positivity (or, at a minimum, acceptance) will spread to every member of the family.

Involving Kids in Relocation Planning

What is important to your child? Ask, and you'll probably receive more opinions than you know what to do with. Most of the big decisions might be out of your kids' control, but there are many ways to help them be active participants in the process:

- ☐ Helping you research houses online or even coming along on house-hunting trips

- ☐ Choosing which room is theirs and how they want it decorated and set up

- ☐ Picking out their most prized possessions to ride along with them on Moving Day

- ☐ Setting up "friends forever" activities with their closest friends: creating a scrapbook or shoebox of cherished memories, making plans for summer visits, etc.

- ☐ Picking out sports and activities to sign up for in the new location

- ☐ Creating a calendar of important dates and activities

- ☐ Keeping a journal of their thoughts and feelings throughout the move

You can also take this opportunity to think about some benefits to the move. What if the new house had a yard big enough that you could get a puppy, or a swimming pool? Are there local summer camps and activities to sign up for, so your child can have fun meeting new friends? Or, for older children, are there good opportunities to pursue their interests and talents?

You know your kids best, so use your best judgment—just remember that, even when you're feeling busy and overwhelmed, you are each oth-

er's best support network. Be there for your young ones, and let them be there for you—like teammates are.

As long as we're together

Candy, Mark, and their two boys had just started to feel at home in their new city–and then Candy was transferred again. They had just a few weeks to pack it all up, and there wasn't enough time to find a new place to live. Despite all the change, this family chose to look on the bright side. Mark's parents lived close to their new location, and the family hatched a plan to show up on the grandparents' doorstep without warning and surprise them. Mark's parents were delighted and even put the whole family up for a few weeks while they found a new house.

Talking to Other Family

Once your nuclear family begins planning together as a team, the rest should be somewhat easier. Your own parents, siblings, and other family members, like you, are adults. If you're moving farther away from them, they may be disappointed; but if you believe in your decision to relocate, they will probably understand and support you. If, like many people, you're moving toward a great opportunity, it's likely that your family will be quite excited and proud! Again, open communication is key: tell your family what to expect, when, and why.

Our relocation experts often work with families who have relied on Grandma and Grandpa for supplementary child care, or who themselves care for elder parents. In these cases, saying goodbye isn't so simple; but you do have a variety of options. Again, take stock of your priorities as you decide what to do. **Nothing can replace a family network—and nothing needs**

to. Thanks to technology, family members will be just a video chat away when you move.

It's very common for grandparents and relatives to come visit the new home and help you unpack. This is a great way for your family to support you in your relocation, while easing the transition. Think to the future. Setting up reunions—whether for holidays, birthdays, or summer vacations—keeps everyone looking forward to the good times ahead.

Shellye's Tip: Everyone has a role to play

When we moved from Maryland to Connecticut, we sat the kids down around the table and told them it was time to relocate. My daughter immediately started to cry. Her younger brother then took his cue from her, and both kids started sobbing. We worked through it as a family, but two years later when we moved again, I did things differently. I told my daughter first, alone. She cried, called friends, and then came back after a couple of hours, saying, "Okay, I've dealt with it."

"Great," I replied. "Now go tell your brother." Because she had already processed the information, she helped him process it too—and he was completely excited to move.

Several years later, my daughter was in high school and my son was in junior high, in Dallas, when I got a new job in California. I had always told my kids that moving was part of our lifestyle, but that when they got to high school, they could choose whether they wanted to stay or go. My daughter chose to stay, and for the next three years I commuted from California to Texas every week, while my husband stayed behind with the kids.

I told my family that, even though I was far away, they could call me any time they needed me and, unless something very important was going on, I would always pick up the phone. Then my daughter surprised me with the gift of a journal that we could pass back and forth, week to week, to write down our thoughts and feelings for each other, even when we weren't able to talk. I believe it even made us closer with each other.

There is no way my family could get through all these re-locations without each and every one of us being involved and committed. Everyone does have a role to play, and we all take care of each other. It's so important to keep the lines of communication open, be accessible to your family, and honor their needs and feelings, even when you're busy or far away.

Smart Moves

Get On the Same Team.

Relocation can bring your family closer together, if you work together. Recognize and talk about everyone's wishes and needs, and commit to helping each other with everything that needs to be done. No matter how big or small, everyone has a role to play!

Be Honest and Straightforward.

Open, honest communication is the key to a successful family move. Don't hide your plans from the kids. Talk openly about your feelings, hopes, and fears too. The more you keep the lines of communication open, the better you'll all work together.

Kids Activity: My Moving Timeline

Print out this sheet at www.ThisSideUpGuide.com and hang it on the fridge or next to the calendar. Fill in important dates, events, and activities. Cross each box off as it is completed.

Family Activity: I'm Feeling...

Give each child (and maybe each parent?) a copy of the emojis on the next page and ask him or her to circle all the emotions he or she is feeling. Talk about what each emotion feels like and how our feelings can change from day to day.

Check in with your child regularly, or whenever he or she is feeling overwhelmed. Which emotions are taking control? Remind your child that every emotion is okay and perfectly natural.

Activity: Family Check-In

No matter how busy things get, there is always time to check in with the most important people in your life. Print out copies of this sheet at www. ThisSideUpGuide.com for every member of the family to help you quickly, and truthfully, understand each other's feelings and priorities.

Name:

What's most important to me right now:

_____

_____

_____

_____

_____

I am most excited about:

_____

_____

_____

_____

_____

I am worried about:

_____

_____

_____

_____

_____

Today I want to:

_____

_____

_____

_____

_____

3. Plan It Out

How to get organized and get moving!

It's time. You've made smart decisions about your priorities; talked with your family and friends; and hopefully had a little time to get excited about what the future holds. Now, you need to start planning for how you'll get there.

Now is the moment to put on your project management hat. Planning a move is just like coordinating any other big project: the more organized you are on day one, the better your outcome will be.

What happens if you *don't* get organized from the get-go? In our experience, the people who don't plan their moves often find themselves in uncomfortable positions. *Wasn't somebody supposed to get the power turned on in our new house? How are we going to fit all these boxes into that truck?* A lack of planning can turn the excitement of starting a new life into stress and confusion. It can also make the days in between much more difficult, as you struggle to figure out what is supposed to happen next.

The information in this chapter will take you from Point A to Point B. We'll give you our very best advice, collected from experts with decades of experience coordinating successful moves. We'll also give you the tools you need to take control and make your plan. The first half of this chapter walks you through the planning process, and the second half is designed to help you keep track of each step.

You'll probably spend more time in this chapter than any other, from now through Moving Day. So let's get started—there's no time to waste!

Trouble saying goodbye to your possessions?

"It really is a grieving process. It physically hurts; you cry. And then, if you're smart, you say, 'It's just a thing.'"

Sue has relocated six times in twenty years, and still remembers the pain of saying goodbye to a favorite antique, because there simply wasn't a place for it in her new house. Still, she's a realist:

"I have an aunt who lost everything to fire twice in her life—but nobody was hurt. It makes you think: when it comes down to it, it's only stuff…It's hard to let go of anything, I don't care if it's anger or a piece of furniture. But we make things so much harder in our own minds than they're actually going to be."

A Word About Time

Some of you reading this book will have months to plan your move; others might only have weeks. Yes, you *can* successfully relocate in just a few weeks' time, though there may be a few challenges (such as the time required to sell your home).

The timeline in this book is based on the six-week period we see most commonly. If you have more (or less) time, adjust your schedule accordingly. Accelerated moves are our speciality; we'll get you through it in style. Above all, if you're worried about getting everything done on schedule, make your plan and stick to it. A solid timeline is your best friend right now.

That said, this is also an important time to keep talking to your real-life friends: those supportive people who will lend an ear and, perhaps, a helping hand when you need it. Sometimes, in all the excitement, it's good to just sit down and talk about what's going on. It is important to find time to de-stress, and it's worth every second!

Talking to your insurance agent about relocating

Ask your agent about:

1. Coverage for damage or theft during the move, or while your vehicle is in storage;

2. Coverage for liability and property damage while you are driving a rental truck, towing a car, or hauling a trailer;

3. Referrals to colleagues in your new location;

4. Any changes to your rates when you move;

5. A supplemental policy for precious or valuable items;

6. Proof of insurance, if needed;

7. Road insurance, if you're driving.

What You'll Need

- **A calendar.** To help you visualize your move, mark your move date, and then cross out all the days when you're unavailable to work on moving. Now you can see exactly how much time you've got to work with, so you can plan accordingly. Use a paper calendar or a shared web calendar to keep everyone in your household up-to-date with the moving schedule. If using a paper calendar, hang it in a central spot where it'll be a common sight.

- **A folder, notebook, or manila envelope.** This can be digital or physical, but you need a "control center" for keeping track of all your important records. In this folder, you will store *everything* related to the move—from your moving checklist, to expenses and receipts, to phone numbers and reminders. Make sure you've got at least one enclosed pocket or envelope for small paper receipts. Even if you're mostly managing your move online, there will be items you simply don't want to lose!

- **A file box, shoebox, or lockbox.** Gather all your documents—including birth certificates, marriage licenses, professional certifications, and reference letters for jobs—and keep them with you. This box will travel with you on the road, so you don't risk losing access to an important document during those crucial moving days. Depending on the value of what you're carrying, make sure this box is appropriately secure, and possibly insured (and make sure you always know where it is).

- **Special boxes for each family member.** Everyone has their own prized possessions. Set up a box for everyone in the household, to be filled with the most important items. For kids, this might be a favorite stuffed toy, or it might be a list of friends' phone numbers. For adults, it might be your favorite job interview ensemble. These boxes can make the trip with you, so you'll have what you need no matter what.

- **(Optional) moving apps.** There are many moving, organizing, checklist, and inventory apps available for your phone, and more are being created all the time. If you live on your phone, consider setting up all your information in an app that you can access wherever and whenever you need it.

The harsh truth about saying goodbye

We all cope with goodbyes in our own way. Angela noticed that, a few weeks before they moved, her ten-year-old daughter suddenly had a big falling out with a friend. Her theory: it's hard to say goodbye, so the girls had to find a way to break their bond and make it easier.

It's not unusual to have emotional outbursts, especially for kids, but for grownups too. The relocation process can look a lot like grieving: you have to bid farewell to your friends, familiar surroundings, your home, and your comfort zone. It simply isn't easy to do, for anyone.

Creating Your Schedule

This checklist is our expert advice on how to plan your relocation, from the first day to Moving Day. We've included everything you likely need to think about. Make a copy of this checklist for your notebook, and add tasks to specific days on your calendar. Be sure to fill in any additional to-do items that pop up!

Six Weeks (Or More) Before Moving Day

- **Connect with real estate agents.** If you're a homeowner, one of your biggest areas of focus will be your property: selling the existing home, and finding a new one in your new area. Waste no time putting these gears into motion. For more information, see the chapters on buying and selling your home.

- **Pre-qualify for a home loan.** Your home buying process will go much more quickly if you are pre-qualified, so start connecting with a lender now.

- **Research the new community.** Refer back to your top priorities as you look at various neighborhoods and communities. Are you most interested in finding good schools? Having a short commute? Seeking out a walkable neighborhood? Whatever your priorities are, make sure you keep them in mind throughout the process.

- **Plan a house-hunting trip.** This is a perfect time to visit your new town, learn your way around, and view some properties. You'll want to determine which neighborhoods are best for you (see the chapter on home buying), as well as what you can expect to afford in the new area. Especially for families with kids, going on a fun visit to the new place can get everyone excited for the future. Try to schedule in some sightseeing and activities, too.

- **De-clutter, sell, and donate.** Now is the time to purge any possessions you don't want to transport. While you may be moving into a home of the same size (or even a larger one), this doesn't mean you'll want to keep all the old things. Hold a yard sale for a little extra cash, or donate your goods to charity for a tax write-off. Whenever possible, avoid the extra work of having to pack and unpack unwanted things!

- **Research storage options.** There are many reasons to consider putting some of your possessions into storage. Perhaps this move isn't permanent, or you will be living in temporary housing for some time. Maybe you'd like to move some things out of your house before Moving Day, to make it easier to stage the home for selling. Whatever your needs, putting items in storage can be a highly effective solution.

- **Hire moving help or make Moving Day plans.** Will you hire a moving company, or rent your own moving van? What will your exact moving dates and times be? Do you want to hire support for jobs like cleaning the house, packing and unpacking, or moving furniture? Put all these details into place ahead of time, so you can schedule around them and budget for costs.

- **Set a relocation budget.** Now that you know the price of moving support, budget for other costs including moving supplies, transportation, temporary housing, and items you'll need in your new home. Remember to keep track of your expenses and save receipts; some moving costs are tax deductible!

- **Begin packing.** It really does help to do a little at a time. Procure your moving boxes, and start filling them. You may wish to schedule specific dates to pack each room, or packing sessions for the whole family.

Four Weeks Before Moving Day

- **Settle your housing arrangement.** You should know where you're moving, whether it's temporary housing or a newly purchased home, by this point. If you don't have this information yet, go for temporary housing or, if possible, consider delaying your move.

- **Notify the appropriate entities of your address change.** Keep track here and don't forget to add any companies or people not on this list.

  ☐ Post Office (change of address form)

  ☐ Banks

  ☐ IRS

  ☐ Department of Veteran Affairs

☐ Social Security Administration

☐ Voter registrar

☐ Credit card companies

☐ Attorneys and accountants

☐ Health insurance providers

☐ Vehicle loans

☐ Previous employer

☐ Children's schools or daycares

☐ Service providers (babysitters, house cleaners, etc.)

☐ Anyone who may need to send you a final invoice after you move

☐ Your alma mater

☐ Magazines and other subscription providers

- **Begin putting items into storage.** Anything you won't be taking with you is probably something you can live without; begin storing these items to free up more room for your move.

- **Give notice.** If you're a renter, give your landlord 30 days' notice in writing. Confirm any conditions required to have your deposit refunded. If you need to break your lease, check in with your local Tenants' Union to find out how best to comply with local regulations and requirements. You may also need to give 30 days' advance notice with service providers, employers, and other professional relationships.

- **Coordinate school, childcare, and/or elder care registration.** Give the previous facility a few weeks' notice in order to arrange record transfers. Contact the new facility to find out about registration and admissions requirements, important dates, etc. If appropriate, add these dates to your calendar.

- **Gather medical records.** Contact doctors, dentists, veterinarians, and other health providers. Let them know you'll be leaving, and request a copy of your records. Ask for paper copies of any prescriptions, to add to your folder.

- **Service vehicles.** Prepare for the trip by having tires rotated, oil changed, and any other appropriate service; or, if you're having your vehicles shipped, arrange for shipping.

- **Check into moving deductions.** Call your accountant or review IRS publication 521 to learn more about current tax deductions for relocation.

- **Talk to your insurance agent about relocation coverage.** See sidebar on page 51 for more detail.

- **Document your valuables and electronics.** Photograph or videotape your valuable possessions; if they are very valuable, have them appraised. Write down serial numbers for your electronic devices.

- **Arrange for your pets' travel.** If you can't take your pets with you, contact a pet mover to set up their travel plans and find out what will be needed for their transport.

- **Plan a goodbye party.** Don't forget to celebrate! Contact friends, kids' friends, and family in the area to set up a get-together. If sending official invitations or electronic invites, ask invitees to reply with their full contact information as well, to make it easier for you to stay in touch.

Two Weeks Before Moving Day

- **Confirm everything.** Go over every detail and make sure it's all going smoothly; if anything is not proceeding according to plan, you've still got time to get back on track.

- **Arrange any final inspections and repairs on your house.** If you haven't yet, make sure your old home is in tip-top shape—before you leave the area.

- **Plan your trip.** Map your route and make any necessary reservations along the way.

- **Help kids plan.** Encourage your children to get together with friends for fun activities; keep a journal of the move; and gather important pictures, memories, and mementos.

- **Wrap up loose ends.** Return library books and things you've borrowed. Pick up things you've loaned, dry cleaning, and sent out for repair.

- **Transfer services.** Call the utility, cable, and other service companies to move your services to the new location.

- **Arrange Moving Day childcare.** Talk to a friend or family member about watching your children on Moving Day, preferably at their home.

- **Transfer prescriptions.** Acquire enough of any prescribed medication to last at least two weeks. Contact a pharmacy in the new area to take over prescriptions, or reach out to a mail-order pharmacy for shipping to the new address.

- **Prepare pets to move.** Find out what shots, papers, and other preparation your pets will need. Take pets to the vet for checkups and to acquire any necessary medication for keeping them calm. Make sure you have ID tags and carriers for each pet.

- **Skimp on groceries.** How much food can you eat from your cupboards? Lighten the load by making meals using the ingredients on hand. Begin donating non-perishables.

- **Finish packing.** Leave only the items you really need, and pack the rest. Empty lesser-used rooms completely.

- **Collect contact information.** Make sure you know how to stay in touch with friends, family, churches, and other groups—especially those who aren't on social networks.

- **Get together with your buddies.** Make time to make memories. Saying goodbye face-to-face, even if it's just a brief visit, leaves everyone feeling positive.

One Week Before Moving Day

- **Confirm Moving Day support.** Call the movers, cleaners, babysitter—anyone you're counting on to make your move go smoothly—and confirm they'll be exactly where you need them to be, when you need them.

- **Gather move-out supplies.** Put together a kit including a hammer, wrench, screwdriver, and other small tools; baggies for saving hardware; tape; and markers. Arrange for food and refreshments for your move-day crew. Make sure you have all the dollies and furniture pads you'll need, and consider acquiring a back brace if you're moving your own furniture. Keep these handy for your move in too!

- **Make your "open first" box.** Pack a box with the absolute essentials: coffee, first aid, toys for the kids, cleaning supplies, and hand tools. Make sure it goes on the truck last!

- **Do your chores.** Clean the house, including appliances, walls, and so on; do any needed yard work; disassemble furniture; and pack anything remaining that you can live without for a few days.

- **Go to the bank.** Withdraw some cash as needed; if your mover requires a registered check, get that too. Empty safe deposit boxes.

- **Get rid of what you can't take.** You can't move or travel with hazardous items such as gas cans and flammable chemicals. Things like houseplants also won't make the journey. Give away and dispose of everything that won't go into the truck.

- **Share your plans with a trusted friend.** Give a friend or family member your itinerary and route.

Day Before Moving Day

- **Do laundry.** Nobody wants to move dirty clothes!

- **Drop off the kids with the sitter.**

- **Rest.** Give yourself a breather, if you can, and a good night's sleep.

Moving Day

- **Clear out the house.** Strip the beds, empty trash cans, and remove towels and incidentals.

- **Do a walk-through.** Check every room, including basements, attics, and sheds.

- **Secure your valuables.** Make sure you know where your most important possessions will be.

- **Pack the truck (or supervise packing).** Whether or not you're using movers, pay attention to how the truck is being loaded. If you've hired movers, supervise their inventory tracking to be sure it's accurate.

- **Keep copies of all receipts and paperwork.** Simply tuck everything into your notebook or file box, to be sorted later.

- **Stay calm!** You've taken care of everything, and now is the time to breathe a little easier. Keep yourself hydrated and take breaks.

Host a camp-in!

With the house in boxes and furniture in storage, it's a perfect opportunity for kids to have friends over for "camping." With more open space to play and fewer knickknacks to knock over, kids can play games like hide-and-seek in the house—or turn down the lights and tell ghost stories.

Shellye's Tip: Divide, conquer…and celebrate.

Moving is a lot of work. It can be really daunting, especially if you haven't done it before, or if it's been a while. Make sure you don't approach this alone. Start by getting help wherever it may be available: from service providers, friends, family, and so on.

My husband and I work best when we divide and conquer. We look at the list, decide who's going to do what and by when…then we split up and handle it. Make sure the work is fairly distributed in a way that it can all get done, and set deadlines so you don't get overwhelmed at any stage.

For kids, this whole process can get old really fast. It's about to take up all your attention and time, and they can feel neglected when everything is about the move (this is true for adults, too). So schedule some times to celebrate or acknowledge your progress. You could use them as rewards—"If we can get these five things done this week, we'll go to the water park"—or simply add them to your to-do list. Just don't forget to have some fun!

Smart Moves

Stay Organized!

We can't say this enough: do whatever it takes to get organized from the outset. Make use of whatever systems, apps, and calendars work best for you. The best way to avoid becoming overwhelmed is to have a clear schedule of what needs to be done and when.

Divide and Conquer.

Even if you're moving solo, but especially if you've got family members old enough to pack boxes, divvy up the work between as many people as possible. Make sure each member of your household has a list of tasks he or she can reasonably accomplish, considering schedule and availability. If it's too much for any of you to handle, consider hiring help or asking friends, family, and community members for support.

PART TWO

Preparing To Move

4. Selling Your Home

What to expect, and what to do

Relocation is a complex equation full of variables—and there is no bigger X factor than the sale of your existing home. After all, it's probably the largest possession you've got! Before your house sells, it can be hard to free up the funds to buy a new one, and this can slow your momentum. But once you sell, there's nothing holding you back—in fact, you'll have just a few weeks to move into the next phase of your life (and hopefully, your new dream home).

It's a lot of change, and it's tough to plan for. In this chapter, we'll give you our experts' best advice for how to approach the sale of your home, how to prepare for the possibilities, and, of course, how to seek your best outcome.

It's important to note that your realtor is the true expert on selling your home; this book won't give you specific, locally focused, or legally actionable guidance in the way your own agent can. What we *do* offer is the experience of guiding people through this process for decades: we've seen it all, and we can tell you what works for most people. So combine the advice in this chapter with your agent's recommendations. We hope the outcome is a happy one!

"Move out" before you move out

When Carrie took a new job hundreds of miles away, Chris knew he didn't want to waste time waiting for their house to sell. Every day they waited for the sale was a day they'd have to be apart, and they preferred to be together. So they put most of their furniture into storage, repainted the entire home, and put it on the market at slightly below the average expected price.

"I set the dining table, and then we ate on the couch," Carrie says. "We didn't touch anything after our house was staged. We wanted everything to be clean and welcoming, so that anybody who walked in could picture themselves living there."

The result: three bids in less than two weeks, and the family spent only a couple of weeks apart before Chris was able to rejoin Carrie in their new location.

It's More Than a House...

It's a home. Whether you've lived in the same place for three years or three decades, your home is a refuge from the world. Countless memories are stored within its walls. It's normal, especially for people who haven't relocated often or recently, to feel sadness about leaving your home.

If a part of you wishes you could just pack up the entire house and take it with you, you're not alone. How can you say goodbye while celebrating all the good memories? For some, a "house cooling" party is a good way to start. For others, it helps to begin depersonalizing the house, packing up the memories along with the possessions and decor.

If you're moving with children, they may have never known another bedroom. Depending on your child's personality, they might be glad to hear that you can set up the new room in just the same way, with the same possessions. Or it might be best to spark their creativity by asking them what they might want in a new house and a new room. By involving your kids in the planning process, you help them feel the excitement of a new beginning, while allowing them to fully experience their emotions around saying goodbye.

What's Your Priority?

Everyone goes into this process a little differently. Your wants and needs can vary greatly, depending on the situation you're in. Are you trying to sell the house as quickly as possible, so you can make an offer on the perfect new home? Or, do you have plenty of time to make repairs and fix up the property to bring in higher bids? Are you willing to redecorate and stage your home, or would you rather keep things as they are until your house sells? Your answers to these questions, and your approach to this process, will have big effects on your outcome.

For the majority of home sellers, the biggest priorities are to get the home sold relatively quickly, and to get as much as possible for the sale price. However, these two goals don't always go hand in hand. Be honest with yourself and your household: what's truly more important for you? What will give you the most momentum as you start your new life? What choices can you make now that will help you stick to the priorities you set at the start of this book?

With all that in mind, it's time to bring in a realtor. As you interview real estate agents, look for someone who clearly wants your business; who knows your area; and who comes well recommended through friends, neighbors, colleagues, or a relocation company. Talk to your realtor about your goals, ask lots of questions, and listen to his or her responses. Will this agent help you get what you want out of the deal?

Ask your agent to take you on a tour of other homes for sale in your area. Look at other homes in the price range you want to sell your home for, as well as homes in your immediate neighborhood. Doing this can help you see what your competition is up to. It can also help you under-

stand what your home is actually worth on the current market, and how to make it appeal to buyers.

You can also ask your agent to do a Buyer's Market Analysis (BMA) of your home, to see how it compares to others in the area. This will give you a good idea of the best price and recommended repairs and upgrades, so your home will be more likely to sell.

"Relocation Beige"

Have you heard of Relocation Beige? It's not an actual color, but this phrase refers to repainting your home in a neutral shade when you're truly motivated to sell. Staging your home—preparing it cosmetically for viewings—can not only help you sell quickly; it can also bring in more and higher bids.

The concept behind staging your home is simple: think of your house as a product for sale. In order to sell it, you want to make it appeal to as many potential buyers as possible. So, while you may love your lime green accent wall and your collection of framed sports jerseys, your unique decorating taste can actually steal attention from the house itself.

In staging your house, your goal is to allow viewers to imagine themselves living there. That generally means toning down your own personal touches. The staging process involves specific steps, including:

- Decluttering and removing knickknacks, personal effects, even furniture and decorations

- Repainting (bonus: this also makes your home smell new)

- Replacing carpets and worn flooring

- Cleaning up the yard and increasing curb appeal

- Renting furniture, if you've already moved out

A good real estate agent will advise you on exactly what you need to do. Take his or her advice! (Oh, and don't take any suggestions personally—trust the professional). In addition, ask for professional photography once your home is staged; since most people shop for real estate online, high-quality photos can make your listing stand out.

When It All Moves Too Fast (Or Slow...)

Relocating is, without exception, an intense and exciting time. It can go incredibly quickly, especially in the beginning when you're making a lot of important decisions in a very short period of time. If you're relocating for a job opportunity, the excitement can be compounded by the need to report to work as soon as possible!

In order to keep up, you'll need to stay in motion. Gain momentum early by starting to take care of the little things right away. When we say you should start packing and decluttering right away, we mean it! It won't just help you say goodbye and make your home more buyer-friendly; it will also keep you on track so you can meet your own deadline comfortably.

However, no matter how fast everything seems to be moving, selling your home is never going to be an instant process. Even after a deal is made, the thirty- to forty-five-day escrow period means you'll be waiting at least a month before the funds change hands. The average home sale takes a few months, and in a slow real estate market, or if you are waiting for a top dollar offer, it can potentially take much, much longer.

What happens when you've staged your home, made relocation plans, started shopping for a new home—and you're not getting any potential buyers for your old house? Suddenly, all that momentum comes to a screeching halt. It's tough (and frustrating) to coordinate a relocation if one of the big key pieces isn't falling into place. If you find yourself treading water, talk to your agent about possibilities to speed up the sale—or consider finding temporary housing in the new area, so you can move ahead (roughly) as planned.

If you find yourself dragging your feet or resisting the idea of leaving your home, be honest about your feelings. Remember, nobody is forcing you to relocate; your plans should be the best choice for your priorities. Communicate openly with your household about what you're feeling, and find the right solution!

Make the tough choices

John and Lisa worked hard to get their house staged just right, but still didn't get any offers on it. They couldn't afford two mortgage payments and needed John's income to continue to cover their expenses. They temporarily separated and Lisa moved into temporary housing in the new location alone and started work, while John stayed behind.

The couple was frustrated during this period of separation because they felt they had control over so little – struggling to find a job long distance as well as the challenge of selling their house. After a couple months, they made the difficult decision to lower their asking price, and a while later, the house eventually sold.

While they didn't get as much money as they were hoping for from the sale of their house, John was finally able to move to the new location, which definitely helped their relationship. They decided to rent a smaller place for a short period to accommodate their current income until John found a new job.

This was a difficult journey for John and Lisa, but in many ways this turned out to be a blessing, because they were able to learn the new area before buying a new place and later found a great fit for them and their lifestyle.

Budgeting and Finances

How much should you ask for your home? What will your closing costs be? What can you expect to pay for your next home? This book won't give you specific financial advice, but we can give you some good tools to help you understand those all-important numbers.

Understanding and budgeting for your closing costs will save you from surprises. Expect to pay anywhere from five to ten percent of the price of your home, depending on where you live and what work your home might need. Closing costs include items such as:

- Realtor fees / commissions

- Loan payoff costs, which may be a little higher than the remaining balance on your loan due to prorated interest

- Transfer taxes or recording fees for transferring the title

- Title insurance fees

- Attorney fees

- Prorated property taxes and homeowner association dues

- Home warranty premium

- Repairs and remediations

- Costs of cosmetic repairs and work done to make your home sale-ready

Your realtor's commission will likely be the largest expense of your relocation (another reason to choose the right agent!). The next largest line item, for many people: your mover's fee.

If you plan to use a moving company, it's a good idea to find it early on. Not only will this help you create a reliable budget, but many moving companies can provide additional help before your actual moving day. They may be able to help you remove your non-essential items, keeping them in storage to free up space in your home. It's possible to find a mover who will bring you storage pods to fill as you pack, or even a storage unit you can access freely.

At the end of this chapter, you'll find a worksheet to help you plan your moving costs. Be sure to review your finances and budget with your accountant or financial planner; our guidelines can't provide you the detailed, custom outlook you truly need, but a professional probably can. The more you can predict at the outset of your move, the more control you'll have over your outcome!

All in all, selling your home is one of those experiences that require you to go with the flow. Many of the factors truly will be outside your control. As always, you *can* control your reaction to the things that are happening—and you can control how you plan for the future post-sale.

So then, determine your budget, find the right realtor and moving support, and take their advice; the rest is just a matter of time.

Who holds the purse strings?

James and Sarah had been married a year or two, but had never had a joint bank account. However, when they moved, they realized they'd be living on a single income while Sarah found work. Creating a joint account helped remove any inequality around household finances, so they felt like teammates and partners during the first stressful months.

Shellye's Tip: Move toward the future, not away from the past

Many of the places I've lived, I've loved—and even after having seventeen different homes throughout my life, I know the pain of leaving a wonderful home is always something I'll feel. You've got to look back, remember the good times, and enjoy those memories. Then, look toward the next adventure. Keep in mind that you're moving toward your future. It's okay to be sad, but there will be happy times ahead.

When staging our home to sell, I try to make it look like a model showroom. I start by taking down family pictures, and decluttering everything. I tell the kids to put everything they want to have available in the next six weeks on their beds, then we put the rest in storage. This helps the house look bigger and brighter, it's a lot easier for us to keep it clean, and most importantly, it helps potential buyers see themselves living there. They don't see our family's home—they see a home they could be happy in.

Once we've done all of this and the house goes on the market, there's usually a lot of activity in the first week. We like to reward ourselves for all our hard work by going away during the open houses and buyer visits. Even if it's only for a weekend, we get out of town. It's something to look forward to, and something we can enjoy together.

Smart Moves

Be Realistic.

Do you want to get top dollar for your home, or do you want to sell quickly? Revisit your priorities and be honest with yourself about what is truly important. What can you do to get what you really want out of your home sale?

Trust the Experts.

An experienced real estate agent can tell you exactly what it will take to sell your home. Sometimes their suggestions will surprise you. Don't take anything personally, just take their advice. If you trust your realtor, you can trust they have your best interests in mind.

Start Packing Now.

Packing extra items early has many benefits: it helps you start the moving process early, it makes your house look more welcoming to potential buyers, it helps you keep things clean and neat—and it gives you a chance to assess what you have and what you want to keep. We urge you to start packing up those knickknacks right away!

Worksheet: What Will It Cost to Move?

Use this worksheet to estimate what you can afford, and what you will earn from the sale of your home. Don't forget to consult with a financial advisor too—these items are only estimates!

1. What are your estimated fixed costs?

$_____   Amount you plan to pay for a new home

$_____   Realtor closing fees

$_____   Moving and storage company fees (see Moving & Storage worksheet)

$_____   Cleaning and repairs

$_____   Final utility bills

$_____   Utility deposits

$_____   Property taxes

$_____   Additional costs

$_____   **Total**

2. What will it cost to physically move the people and animals in your family?

Research the cost of various modes of transportation to discover the best solution.

Car Travel

$_____ Fuel

$_____ Lodging

$_____ Meals

$_____ Pet transportation and/or lodging

$_____ Additional expenses

$_____ **Total**

Air Travel

$_____ Airline tickets

$_____ Lodging

$_____ **Total**

Meals

$_____ Pet transportation and/or lodging

$_____ Car shipping

$_____ Additional expenses

$_____ **Total**

Bus or Train Travel

$_____ Bus or train tickets

$_____ Lodging

$_____ Meals

$_____ Pet transportation and/or lodging

$_____ Car shipping

$_____ Additional expenses

$_____ **Total**

3. What are your supply costs?

$_____ Moving boxes

$_____ Furniture and mattress pads

$_____ Packing materials (newspaper, bubble wrap, tape, markers)

$_____ Moving day refreshments and supplies

$_____ Additional expenses

$_____ **Total**

4. Do you have additional income or profits?

$_____ Estimated profits from the sale of your home

$_____ Relocation financial assistance from your employer

$_____ Payout from employer for extra vacation time, etc.

$_____   Sale of a spare car

$_____   Sale of extra furniture or belongings

$_____   Additional profits

$_____   **Total**

5. Add it all up.

$_____   Total fixed costs (Step 1)

$_____   Total travel costs (Step 2)

$_____   Total supply costs (Step 3)

$_____   _____

$_____   **Expense subtotal**

$_____   Incidental costs (multiply subtotal by ten percent)

$_____   _____

$_____   **Total expenses**

$_____   Total income or profit (Step 4)

$_____   _____

$_____   **Total costs**

Worksheet: Researching Moving & Storage Companies

Use this worksheet to keep track of your research while you find the right moving and/or storage service providers.

Moving Services

Get estimates from at least three moving companies. Ask about fees for extra services, like storage, piano moving, or professional packing, and taxes or surcharges. Also request references who will speak to the professionalism of the company's services.

Company 1: _____

Phone/email: _____

Cost: _____

Notes: _____

_____

_____

_____

Company 2: _____

Phone/email: _____

Cost: _____

Notes: _____

_____

_____

_____

Company 3: _____

Phone/email: _____

Cost: _____

Notes: _____

_____

_____

_____

Rental Trucks

If desired, research at least two options for renting your own moving truck. Ask about the cost for any relevant accessories, such as tow dollies or car carriers. Also ask about each truck's fuel economy, then calculate the cost of fuel.

Company 1: _____

Phone/email: _____

$_____   Truck rental

$_____   Accessories

$_____   Fuel cost

$_____   **Total**

Company 2: _____

Phone/email: _____

$_____   Truck rental

$_____   Accessories

$_____   Fuel cost

$_____   **Total**

Company 3: _____

Phone/email: _____

$_____   Truck rental

$_____   Accessories

$_____ Fuel cost

$_____ **Total**

Storage

If your moving company will not provide your storage, research at least three storage facilities. Visit storage units in person and take note of security, cleanliness, and ease of access.

Company 1: _____

Phone/email: _____

Cost: _____

Notes: _____

_____

_____

_____

Company 2: _____

Phone/email: _____

Cost: _____

Notes: _____

_____

_____

_____

Company 3: _____

Phone/email: _____

Cost: _____

Notes: _____

_____

_____

_____

5. Finding Your New Home

How to make a big decision in a short time

Is there anything more exciting than shopping for a new house? Granted, at this stage you may not be looking for more excitement—but nonetheless, with a long list of possible homes, neighborhoods, even towns to choose from, this can easily be the most creative and imaginative part of relocating.

Along with excitement, you might experience a fair dose of fear: *What if we don't find anything we like? What if we pick a bad neighborhood? What if we can't afford something big enough for our family?* There can also be some frustration if, for example, your old home doesn't sell quickly and you miss the opportunity to bid on a wonderful house.

Meanwhile, for those who are relocating across long distances, the biggest challenge by far may be simply finding a home to buy. Particularly if you need to move quickly, you might have just one shot to pick out the new house—talk about an intimidating choice!

Still, with plenty of Internet research and the help of an expert or two, you *can* find a wonderful property; people do it all the time. In fact, this happens to be a speciality of the experts contributing to this book. In this chapter, we'll walk you through the steps needed to find, purchase, and move into your new home with as little stress as possible, under the circumstances.

Don't forget to keep a positive attitude and focus on your top priorities. Now let's go house shopping!

Ask an expert (and keep an open mind!)

When Alan moved to Atlanta, he asked his realtor to help him find a newer condo that allowed pets. After their initial meeting that included her asking Alan more about his lifestyle, he was surprised when she recommended he also view some single-family homes in an older part of town. However, he soon saw the appeal of the charming bungalows in a neighborhood he would not have looked at. Alan found a beautiful brick home on a small lot, and his dog loved having a yard to play in.

What Can You Get?

By the time most people read this chapter, you'll probably be well into your research. But if you haven't yet pulled up a real estate website or app and done some exploring, now is the time! You may or may not actually find *the* house through your own searching. However, this preliminary research will give you lots of highly valuable information, such as:

What types and styles of houses are available in the new area?

Many people hope to find a home that's very similar to what they had before—or they focus on new construction. However, each area has its own style of homes, and it can be beneficial to keep all your options open.

Use the worksheet at the end of this chapter to examine the possibilities, and don't forget to include the whole family!

How much house can you afford?

Your budget is the bottom line, but that doesn't mean you'll find the same thing you had previously: $200,000 might mean something very different in Minnesota than in New York. As you conduct your research, you'll quickly see what you can realistically afford. Be honest about your expectations, and set expectations early with your family too.

It's highly recommended to pre-qualify for your loan. Taking this step sooner than later can help you be ready to bid on the right home as soon as you find it—a big advantage in a competitive market.

Who are the local buyer's agents who might be able to serve as your realtor?

As you peruse homes in the new area, take note of any realtor names that pop up next to the houses you like most. Unless you have been assigned a realtor (as part of a corporate relocation, for example), you want to look for agents who live in the area and are likely to know it well. If you know anyone in the area, ask for recommendations. Make sure you seek out a buyer's agent, rather than a seller's agent who might be more interested in showing you specific properties.

Which neighborhoods, townships, and developments appeal to you?

Do you like to be close to major thoroughfares, or more removed from the city center? Are you seeking a home with a view, or a walkable neighborhood? Are there specific cultural communities you want to seek out? When you're new to an area, it's hard to know what your options are. Seek out the local Chamber of Commerce or Tourist Board to get information on different parts of town, and use information aggregator sites to get details on school districts, crime rates, demographics, and so on. Once you've found a realtor, ask him or her as many questions as you can think of!

Thinking ahead

With Steve needing to report to his new job in three weeks, he and Jenny had just one 48-hour visit to find a home in the Boston area. Thankfully, they had sought out an experienced, motivated realtor who had done her homework. She helped them choose a townhome in a highly sought-after neighborhood. Three years later when the family relocated again, they were able to sell the home extremely quickly.

Go On A Look-See Trip

It's time! You've secured a buyer's agent, done your research, and found a few houses you want to view. Finally, you've got a chance to visit the area that will become your new home.

For many people reading this book, tension will be high at this stage. If you're relocating for a job opportunity, you might only have one chance to choose a new home before you move. The stress can be compounded by any doubts about selling your old house, or disagreements about what you're really looking for.

In order to make this trip go as well as it can, you need three things: a positive attitude, a good realtor, and a great pair of walking shoes. Keep your mind open and see what you find.

Many people prepare for their home-shopping trips by putting together lists of houses they want to see. Before you jump in, however, ask your realtor to give you a tour of the area. You may find that certain neighborhoods are better for your needs. Spend some time talking to your realtor in advance of your tour: ask questions, share your priorities from

the first chapter of this book, and make full use of your agent's local knowledge!

As you view homes, remember the priorities you've set. Use the worksheet at the end of this chapter to help you focus on what is most important to you and every member of your household. If for some reason you don't find what you're looking for, do an honest reassessment of your requirements. Do you need to scale back your expectations to fit your budget? Are you looking for features or property types that aren't commonly available in the new area? Or would you simply prefer to conduct your search more slowly, living in temporary housing while you look for the ideal home? Again, focus on meeting your top priorities, and if needed, prepare to compromise in other areas.

Attitude is truly the key. You have an opportunity to make your life even better than it already is—what types of improvements do you want to make, and how can you make adjustments so you reach your goals?

Share the dream

When Anna's family moved across the country, she knew her daughters would be worried about the big change. So the family brought the girls along for a house-shopping trip. "My youngest was really into swimming pools," Anna says. "She loved every house that had a pool. We knew we weren't going to buy a house with a pool, and told her so, but seeing her get excited about different houses was fun for all of us."

How can you involve every member of your household in the process of saying goodbye to the past and moving toward the future?

The Buying Process

When it comes to buying a home, the process is roughly the same no matter where you go. However, different areas do have slight variations in practices. As just one example: in some parts of the United States, appliances come with the home, while in others they do not.

If you've owned a home before, you shouldn't have too many surprises. Trust your realtor's expertise and ask plenty of questions about each step of the process. Here's a basic overview:

1. **Research.** As detailed above, your first step is to determine exactly what you're looking for.

2. **Contact a realtor.** Choose the expert who will guide you through the process.

3. **Pre-qualify for financing.** As we've mentioned, this is standard practice and a smart idea for making everything go more smoothly.

4. **View homes and make your choice.** As recommended by your realtor, consider choosing a backup as well, so you don't need to make a second trip in case you aren't able to secure your first choice.

5. **Make an offer and negotiate with the seller.** Work with your realtor on this process; he or she will recommend the best offer amount and contract terms to help facilitate a deal that meets your top priorities. That said, never assume that this process will be cut-and-dried; it's quite common to go through a few steps before a deal is reached.

6. **Secure your financing.** Now that you've determined the specifics, return to your lender to finalize your mortgage payment, down payment, and other terms.

7. **Close the deal.** The escrow or settlement process can take several weeks as you complete the final steps, including a title search, home inspections and walkthrough, and the final settlement. Your realtor can shepherd this process for you, and some people also work with a lawyer to ensure the deal is solidly completed.

Enjoy the process

Sue and Tom were delighted to find rare new construction in San Francisco, but the property wouldn't be finished until after their move date. So Tom rented an extended-stay hotel room close to his new office, while Sue took the opportunity for a relaxed cross-country road trip with her dog—something she had always dreamed of doing. While she was crossing off an item from her bucket list, she took photos, visited places she'd always wanted to see, and updated her friends with daily blog posts.

Timing Isn't Everything

Let's be frank: there are a lot of moving parts in a relocation, and it's incredibly difficult to get them all to line up at exactly the right moment. Our experts work with people all the time who are waiting to buy a new home until they sell the old one; living in temporary housing until they can find a home they like; living out of boxes while repairs are finished; and just about any other situation you can think of.

Don't expect the timing of your home sale and purchase—two separate processes that can involve several weeks of waiting periods—to be perfectly timed. Instead, plan to be flexible, so you will be comfortable while the details are sorted out. Many people make use of temporary housing in one form or another: having a "halfway house" to live in for the short term alleviates stress and pressure, allowing you more freedom to make the choices you need, while still moving forward with your relocation.

If you're moving for a job, your company may help with housing costs; however, some temporary housing options can be on the expensive side. If you're covering the cost yourself, look for month-to-month or short-term leased apartments, or even extended-stay hotels. In the long run, a few weeks of living in a hotel is a relatively easy sacrifice to make in exchange for smoother planning and increased options!

If you wind up in a rental or temporary home for more than a few weeks, take the time to research its location. Particularly for families with kids, your temporary home should be located in the same school district where you plan to register them permanently. Other considerations include your commute time, access to grocery stores, walkability, and other details that will make your temporary home a comfortable one.

Again, keep your options open: a great house is worth waiting for, and a few hiccups in planning are to be expected. As long as you are making smart decisions that serve your top priorities, you are making it possible for this relocation to be a successful one.

Shellye's Tip: Know what you want!

My husband and I have never moved into a house and then said, "What were we thinking?" There have been tradeoffs, but always because we chose them. Our first house had long commutes for both of us. That's because our priority was to have kids right away, and we wanted to budget for good childcare. So we set aside the money it would take to hire good caregivers, and bought a house with what was left over. As I drove my long commute, I always reminded myself why it was worth it.

Setting your priorities is paramount when looking for a new home. It's very easy to walk into a house that smells like cookies, is bright and clean, and has a great yard…and you become so captivated, you forget that it's not in a neighborhood you like, etc. Bring a list of what you want and don't, so you can be objective.

We also spend a lot of time researching and interviewing realtors. I'm looking for someone who has been selling homes in the area for eight to ten years, so they really understand some nuances that will help with our search. I also look for a realtor who really listens to us. Once we've made that connection, we spend time to make sure they understand what we're looking for, so they can leverage our time. When you move for a job, you often have to start right away. The more time you spend looking for a place to live, the harder it is to feel settled.

Once we do have a house in mind, I always want to talk to the owners and ask them about the neighborhood. If they can tell me about the other people on the street, that's a neighborhood I want to live in.

Your priorities will be different than mine, but make sure you know what they are, and ask all the questions you need to make sure this home and community are right for you.

Smart Moves

Do Your Homework.

When you move to a new area, you effectively start from scratch. In order to make a smart decision, you'll need to learn a lot about the community, beyond just what houses cost. Research realtors carefully and then educate your realtor on your priorities.

Trust the Experts.

Again, a real estate agent you trust is your greatest ally. Don't just print out a list of houses to visit; ask your agent to make some recommendations. Request a tour of the town. Leverage his or her specialized knowledge to find homes and neighborhoods that truly meet your needs.

Be Objective.

Watch out for house crushes! Always keep in mind your priorities, and no matter how wonderful a house may seem, be sure to evaluate it objectively and be honest about whether it will be a good home.

Activity: Home Is Where The _____ Is

Before you shop for houses in earnest, take the time to fill out this worksheet with your entire household.

What do I/we like about my/our current house?

_____

_____

_____

_____

_____

What don't we like about our house?

_____

_____

_____

_____

What do we like about our current neighborhood?

_____

_____

_____

_____

_____

What don't we like about our neighborhood?

_____

_____

_____

_____

_____

What are our top priorities in this relocation (from Chapter One) and what do they tell us about the types of houses and neighborhoods we should look for?

_____

_____

_____

_____

_____

What are some things we really need this new home to have (if not listed above)?

_____

_____

_____

_____

_____

What are some things it would be really nice to have?

_____

_____

_____

_____

_____

What are we sure we don't want in a new house?

_____

_____

_____

_____

_____

Worksheet: Prepare For Your Home Buying Trip

Use this worksheet to keep track of your progress as needed.

Realtor Research

Jot down names, emails, and phone numbers of realtors you will contact.

_____

_____

_____

_____

Note any questions you want to ask realtors, including information about neighborhoods, schools, commute time, as well as the home buying process in the new area.

_____

_____

_____

_____

Potential Homes

Use this area to keep track of addresses, prices, and notes about any houses you want to visit on your home buying trip.

_____

_____

_____

_____

_____

_____

_____

_____

_____

Other Research

Keep track of any information you discover and questions you have about the new area, such as neighborhood data, crime rates, transportation, culture, and so on.

_____

_____

_____

_____

_____

_____

_____

_____

_____

Loan Pre-Qualification

List the name and contact information of your lender, the amount you are pre-qualified for, and any other notes.

_____

_____

_____

_____

_____

_____

_____

_____

6. Managing Your Stuff

How to take what you need (and ditch what you don't)

If we said that your relationship to your belongings has a lot to do with your life philosophy, would you believe it?

Think about it: do you believe that your happiest times are ahead of you, or behind you? Do you prefer to live simply, or to be surrounded by nice things?

When you're hanging on to things you don't really need, it's probably because they remind you of specific ideas or experiences you'd like to remember, or perhaps bring more of into your life. If you find it easy to stay organized, you may be mentally clearing the way for new opportunities.

(And if every single surface in your house is cluttered…you might have kids.)

Stuff comes into our lives in myriad ways: it sneaks in through the front door, crammed into bags, stashed in pockets, and sometimes packed in shipping boxes. Once stuff has made its way in, it never seems to want to leave. If you've got a drawer full of matchbooks, rubber bands, and packs of gum someplace in your house, you are in the majority.

Stuff is all fine and good until it's time to relocate. Suddenly the reality of years' worth of collected knickknacks looms in front of you. How will you ever deal with it all?

To be perfectly honest, we know that many people end up packing most of their stuff, moving it wholesale, and sorting through it in the new house. If this is your plan, we'd like to recommend something a little more elegant. In this chapter, we'll explore some ways to deal with stuff, including changing your philosophical outlook to allow you to part with a few things. We'll talk about your options for moving and storage. And finally, we'll give you specific information on how to pack for Moving Day.

The sooner you start on this process, the better. So let's dig in.

Kid Stuff

Tania took her family's relocation as an opportunity to help her kids get rid of some of their older clothes and toys. She explained to her sons that not all children had as many toys as they did, and that it would be nice for them to pack up some things they wanted to give to another kid. Her boys kept their favorites, and helped her pack the rest for donation.

There were still a few things that the boys thought they wanted, but Tania knew they hadn't used in some time. She boxed those items separately, several weeks before Moving Day. Anything that the boys wanted to play with came out of the box and was kept. The rest was donated as well.

Who Are You Becoming?

If you want some added inspiration for this process, look no further than *The Life Changing Magic of Tidying Up* by Marie Kondo—a book celebrated for its simple, positive attitude toward simplifying and reducing your stuff. Its core lesson: **instead of deciding what to get rid of, focus on deciding what you want to keep.**

One particularly relevant quote applies directly to the transition that happens when we relocate:

"The space in which we live should be for the person we are becoming now, not for the person we were in the past."

When you relocate, it's a fantastic opportunity to look to the future and welcome a positive change. Who are you becoming? What does that person need to have on hand?

This is what it really means to reflect on your philosophical attitude toward stuff. Granted, it may not be realistic for you to completely overhaul your possessions in the midst of a relocation; that's what storage pods are for. Nonetheless, as you come up against difficult decisions, try to approach them with this attitude: what do you want to bring into your new life?

Space: It's Not Actually Infinite

As soon as you start researching homes in your new area, you should start to have a good idea of how much house you can afford: square footage, layout, and so on. Even at this early stage, you can look realistically at your furniture and start to decide what you really want to bring with you—and what you can possibly leave behind.

In our experience, almost everyone moves with more furniture than they actually need. Even if you are upgrading to a larger house, your old furniture may not suit it; or it may simply be difficult to plan how you'll arrange things until you can actually get them into your new place. While it's easy to think, "I'll just take it all with me and get rid of things later," we don't recommend this. First of all, it costs money to move each piece of furniture. Second, by choosing to be choosy, you can save a lot of time and hassle while giving yourself freedom to evolve.

At the end of this chapter is a House Inventory worksheet you can use to keep track of all your major possessions—furniture in particular—and make decisions about what will happen to them. Start filling it out now, and you'll soon be able to see which items are truly important to your future.

Parting with possessions

Sue knew she was moving to a much, much smaller house, but she couldn't bring herself to get rid of her treasured antique living room set. She went over her plans again and again, trying to find a place for the pieces in her new home. In the end, though, there was no way to make them fit.

Sue cried herself to sleep that night, grieving not only the loss of her favorite pieces, but of the home she had spent the past several years in. In the morning, she was ready. She called up a handyman who had helped her prepare the home for sale, and asked him if he wanted the pieces, which he had always admired. As hard as it was to say goodbye, Sue knew it was "just stuff," and was glad it could bring happiness to someone she appreciated. She didn't charge him a dime for the furniture.

What To Do With Your Stuff (Before Moving Day)

If you're like most people, you probably want to get a head start on your relocation. Removing some of your furniture and possessions from your house is the perfect way to build up a little momentum; and as we've discussed, it's also a great strategy for staging your home to sell quickly.

Removing things from your house generally means you need to store them, sell them, donate them, or dump them. As a general rule, the top two options are storage or donation. However, selling things can take more time than you realistically have, and throwing them away (aside from being wasteful) can cost you dumping fees. Nonetheless, you'll probably incorporate all four options into your plan. Here's a brief rundown:

Storage

This option can be very easy: if you're working with a moving company, the odds are good that they will also offer some storage services. Storage pods, which are delivered to your driveway and then picked up once you've filled them, are an incredibly convenient option. If you want to be able to access your things easily, you can rent a storage unit and fill it however you like. Start scheming early for what you can put into storage, even temporarily. Some people, predicting that they'll relocate again within a few years, will store treasured items until they have space for them again. Whatever your needs, there's likely to be an option to meet them!

Selling

Depending on how much time and financial leeway you have, this process can go several different ways. If you're in a rush, we recommend pricing items to sell quickly; if you want to recoup more of their value, then expect that they will take longer to sell. Local listing sites are the way to go; instead of listing each item separately, list them together as a moving sale. You can also look into consignment shops and even auction houses to help facilitate the process while you focus on all the other things you need to do!

Donation

This calls for a return to your philosophy of stuff: will your possessions bring even greater value to someone in need? By donating to thrift stores, charities, and even neighbors, you can give back (and secure your tax refund) while greatly cutting down the amount of time that would otherwise be required to move or sell things. Consider inviting friends over to "go shopping" in your stuff; they'll appreciate the gesture, and you'll have another excuse to spend time together before you move.

Dumping

When time is tight, sometimes your best (or last) option is to rent a dumpster. This is most likely to coincide with Moving Day, but don't make this your only option! Whenever possible, give your stuff a chance for another life before sending it to the landfill.

Moving overseas?

Diya knew she couldn't bring everything when her family relocated from India to the United States, but she could bring a taste of home. She made sure to pack her pressure cooker and some of the spices that would be hard to find in the United States, so she could have a home-style meal now and then.

With limited luggage space, it can be very difficult to know what you should bring with you on an overseas move; even space for clothing is at a premium. If possible, use message boards to talk with expatriates and other people living in the country you're headed to. Keep the climate in mind, as well as any standards for dress and fashion in the new country.

The Two-Week Box

As you prepare to pack for your move, you should also be planning your "two-week box"—the items you'll need for your first two weeks in the new place. Each member of the household should have his or her own two-week box (or bag), with things like:

- ☐ Essential clothing and toiletries

- ☐ Medications

- ☐ Important papers necessary for employment, school transfers, and so on

- ☐ A professional outfit for job interviews, important meetings, or other potential events

- ☐ Good walking shoes

- ☐ Toys, books, and entertainment for days without Internet or television

- ☐ Kids' comfort items such as favorite blankets, prized possessions, etc.

When creating your two-week box, prepare to be living out of it for longer than you might think. Unforeseen events, miscommunications, and even weather can cause delays; while it's unlikely that you will be without your things for more than a couple of weeks, be prepared for whatever could happen.

With that said, you're not moving out of civilization entirely, and you're likely to have access to stores, banks, pharmacies—and public transportation or cab service to help you reach them, if needed. Items such as pots and pans might seem necessary, but if you don't have room to pack them on the plane, you can pick up a cheap set for temporary use upon arrival. Don't throw in the kitchen sink; stick to the things you really need, and the rest will come to you soon enough.

Packing & Moving Day

First things first: our experts definitely recommend starting your packing process early, and keeping up with it as you go. This helps keep stress low (and organization high) while saving you from having to do all the work at the last minute.

No matter how organized you are, the packing and moving process always takes more time, and more space, than you expect. If you're working with a moving company, follow their recommendations for the size of truck, and the man-hours, they recommend. Even if it seems high, if the company is licensed, bonded, and well-reviewed, you can trust them to know their business.

Begin the process by inventorying your home, using the worksheet in this chapter or by creating your own spreadsheet. Movers will normally create their own inventory list, which you should check carefully before signing. In addition, keep track of your electronics and other items which might become damaged. Photograph valuables, write down serial numbers, and backup computers; this will help you get them replaced if something goes wrong.

If you want certain items to come off the truck first so you can start using them right away, mark them as "pack last" and confirm with the movers. This might include kids' toys, toiletries, bed linens, and other things you'll need sooner than later.

Finally, consider donating your excess food. Organizations such as Move For Hunger can help you identify moving companies that will transport your extra non-perishable, unopened food to local charities and food banks.

Remember that your movers are working very hard to take care of your possessions—a little kindness goes a long way on Moving Day! Have refreshments and snacks on hand, and even though you may be stressed out, treat your movers with kindness and patience. You never know when they might be able to return the favor.

Moving Day will almost certainly be chaotic. Limit distractions by having neighbors or family members watch your kids or pets. Get plenty of rest, and wear clothes and shoes you can lift boxes in. Even if you've planned perfectly, there will be a lot to do and a lot to think about. If something does go awry, just remember that, in the end, everything will most likely work out just fine. Take a break, drink some water, and move on.

Soon enough, you will find yourself at the door of your new home. Time to move in and begin the next stage: creating a happy life full of new experiences and new opportunities—and yes, new "stuff" too.

Shellye's Tip: Be intentional

Moving from Texas to California meant we had to downsize; you get a third of the house for three times the money! It was hard to figure out what to keep and what to get rid of. So we walked through the new place and decided exactly what would go where. Focusing on what to keep is easier than focusing on what to give away: you know that everything you're keeping has a place.

Funny story: when I was a child, the company my father worked for arranged a relocation for our family. It was completely turnkey: they hired the movers, who also packed the house for us. That was great, but when we got to the new place and started unpacking, we found they had packed the garbage bin—full of garbage! It was a terrible smell. We had no idea they would pack absolutely everything. Turnkey or not, there are always decisions you need to make about what you need, and what you absolutely don't.

Over the years, I've learned the art of marking boxes, which can make or break the unpacking process. Mark each box with the room it's coming from, the room it's going to, and a summary of what's inside. This keeps you from opening every box in the house just to find a pair of scissors, and it also helps you get boxes to the right rooms, instead of having a mountain stacked in your living room.

Finally, right before your move, pack three sets of boxes to be opened first. One: a box with all the tools and supplies you'll need for unpacking, such as box cutters, hammers, screwdrivers, picture hangers, etc. Two: pack a full place setting, silverware, cups, coffee maker, and other essentials for the next morning. Three: pack all the bedding together for the family for the first night, instead of putting all the sheets together and so on. Have full sets of bedding, blankets, and pillows readily available, so you can sleep!

Smart Moves

Don't Pack the Kitchen Sink.

Approach your stuff from the attitude of "this is what we have space for and want to keep," rather than trying to figure out what to get rid of. This makes it easier to cut back on your stuff, without getting rid of the things you truly want.

Make a Two-Week Box.

Every member of the family should have a box or bag with enough clothing and other items to get through two weeks. Just in case something goes wrong, or in case you'll be spending a lot of time traveling to your destination, the two-week box means you'll be prepared.

Worksheet: Home Inventory

Use these inventory sheets to keep track of everything. You may wish to print multiple copies of some sheets at www.ThisSideUpGuide.com as needed. Alternatively, you can create your own spreadsheet or even download a home inventory app.

As you inventory your home, take photos of everything. They will be extremely important in the case of any misplaced items or insurance claims. It's better to have photos and not need them, than the other way around!

Living Room

	Original Price	Year of Purchase	Model or Serial No. (if applicable)	Status (Packed/ Stored/Etc.)
Rugs/carpet				
Sofa(s)				
Coffee & side table(s)				
Table & chairs				
Media center				
Shelves				
Curtains/blinds				
Lamps/light fixtures				
Art & wall decor				
Other				

Family Room & Office

	Original Price	Year of Purchase	Model or Serial No. (if applicable)	Status (Packed/ Stored/Etc.)
Art & wall decor				
Rugs/carpet				
Sofa(s)				
Curtains/blinds				
Table & chairs				
Desk				
Bookcase(s)				
File cabinet(s)				
Media center				
Lamps & light fixtures				
Other				

Dining Room

	Original Price	Year of Purchase	Model or Serial No. (if applicable)	Status (Packed/ Stored/Etc.)
Rugs/carpet				
Table				
Chairs				
Other furnishings				
Silverware				
China				
Glassware				

	Original Price	Year of Purchase	Model or Serial No. (if applicable)	Status (Packed/Stored/Etc.)
Tablecloths & napkins				
Art/wall decor				
Lamps & light fixtures				
Other				

Bathroom(s)

	Original Price	Year of Purchase	Model or Serial No. (if applicable)	Status (Packed/Stored/Etc.)
Cabinets/chests				
Mirrors				
Room decor				
Towels				
Clothes hamper				
Medicine cabinet				
Hair dryers/irons				
Electric shaver				
Other				

Kitchen & Laundry

	Original Price	Year of Purchase	Model or Serial No. (if applicable)	Status (Packed/ Stored/Etc.)
Cabinets/shelving				
Table & chairs				
Dishware, flat-ware, & glassware				
Pots & pans				
Clocks & wall decor				
Refrigerator				
Stove				
Microwave				
Dishwasher				
Washer/Dryer				
Small appli-ance(s)				
Other				

Household Electronics

	Original Price	Year of Purchase	Model or Serial No. (if applicable)	Status (Packed/ Stored/Etc.)
Television #1				
Television #2				
Computer/laptop #1				
Computer/laptop #2				

Computer accessories (printer, external hard drives, etc.)				
Speakers/stereo system				
DVD player				
Mobile phone(s)				
Tablet(s)				
Video game systems				
Camera(s)				
Other				

Bedroom(s)

	Original Price	Year of Purchase	Model or Serial No. (if applicable)	Status (Packed/ Stored/Etc.)
Bedframe				
Mattress(es)				
Linens				
Nightstand(s)				
Dresser(s)/armoire				
Jewelry				
Bookcase				
Desk/vanity				
Chair				
Mirror				
Lamps & light fixtures				
Closet accessories				

Clothes & shoes				
Other				

Garage, Basement, Attic, & Outdoors

	Original Price	Year of Purchase	Model or Serial No. (if applicable)	Status (Packed/ Stored/Etc.)
Sports equipment				
Tools				
Lawnmower				
Ladder(s)				
Work bench				
Grill/BBQ equipment				
Patio furniture				
Exercise equipment				
Toys & games				
Trunks & luggage				
Other				

Miscellaneous Inventory

	Original Price	Year of Purchase	Model or Serial No. (if applicable)	Status (Packed/ Stored/Etc.)

PART THREE

Welcome Home

7. Making Friends

How to have fun and fit in

Do you remember the moment when you met your best friend? Did you have any idea, at the time, how important he or she would become to you?

We can never accurately predict how our friendships and relationships will work out—which is just one reason why we recommend you try to meet lots of new people after your relocation. The funny lady from your exercise class, the neighbor with an ATV in the driveway, even the person sitting next to you at a concert…you never know who will be the next bright light to illuminate your life.

What you *should* know is that making new friends is one of the best things you can do for your health and happiness. Research shows that people with active social lives tend to live better and longer. In your own experience, you probably feel better when you've got something interesting to do on the weekend, somebody to play hooky with on a sunny day, and somebody to listen when you need to talk. And while you may still have strong, vibrant friendships that thrive over social media, it's important to have friends you can see in person, too, which will play a big role in making you (and your family) feel at home again quickly.

Our experts find that the people who get out and make friends are also the people who end up happier after six months or a year. You don't have to be an outgoing person to do this; we've got plenty of tips for introverts, too. All that matters is that you give yourself the opportunity to meet people who can make your life more exciting and fun.

You may not have much time to put yourself out there in the first few weeks, while you're unpacking and learning your way around town; but sooner or later, you *will* have some free time (we promise!), and we've got lots of suggestions for how to spend it.

A whole new world

Sun's daughter was just the age to enter kindergarten when they moved to the United States. It was a huge transition: a new culture, a new language, and a new routine. There were many tantrums and tears, which threatened to break Sun's heart—but to her surprise, after only two months, her daughter was completely at home in her new life.

Kids: Your Personal Icebreaker

The younger members of your family, in addition to being wonderful, growing, brilliant people with their own lives to lead, are also your free entry pass to a number of social circles. (Sorry, kids! You might have to go places with Mom for the first couple of months.)

For most parents, getting the kids involved in school and activities is a top priority. You may have chosen your house based on the school district; perhaps you researched local sports, camps, and arts groups to help your kids get excited about relocating. They may even have started a new school or activity within the first couple of weeks after your move.

It's natural for parents to put their children's needs and activities first— not just for their own good, but also to help create a routine and build some excitement into each week. However, don't neglect your own social needs. We commonly see parents spend all their energy making sure everyone in the family is settled and happy, only to discover that they missed the opportunity to make friends of their own.

Seeking out families with kids around the same age as yours is a natural, and obvious, icebreaker. You may find that there are children in your neighborhood, whose parents could have recommendations for fun stuff to do. Don't be afraid to ask what they do for fun, and if they seem friendly, even propose an outing.

It's also easy enough to meet fellow parents at games, rehearsals, and school meetings. Not sure what to say? Try this:

The Three Magic Words

There's one little phrase that will open doors and start conversations wherever you go, and it's something you should have no trouble saying. Feeling shy or unsure of how to begin? Just say:

"I'm new here."

A winning pair

Sue was never very interested in volunteering; whenever she'd show up to a site, she always seemed to end up in charge. Reluctant to join a local group, but eager to meet new people, she decided to look into training classes for her German Shepherd.

Signing up for a group class, Sue quickly discovered that her dog—much like her—was a real go-getter. Not only did she meet fellow dog enthusiasts, but she was soon advancing through the training levels at high speed. In the end, her dog's trainer became one of her closest friends, and the dog became a blue ribbon winner!

There's something about those three little words that triggers people's kindness and welcoming instincts. You'll be amazed at how well it works: utter this phrase, and total strangers will suddenly morph into your cheerleaders and tour guides. At the very least, it will automatically spark a great conversation-starting response: "Oh? Where are you from?"

This is especially effective in group situations, such as baseball games, church gatherings, and networking events. The next time you find yourself in such a situation, try it out. You may not make lifelong friends that very instant, but you might find yourself invited to the next party or event. And that's a strong start.

By the way, while we're talking about the magic words, we should also mention their enemy: a negative attitude. If someone asks you how things are going and you respond with, "I'm really struggling...I can't find anything and I'm so stressed out..." and so on—they are likely to reflect that negative emotion back to you. Remember to stay positive; this creates positive interactions, which turn into positive relationships. You don't have to lie; relocating is hard! Just remember to talk about your hopes, ideas, and accomplishments along with the struggles.

Finding your strength

Eric's son Jayden was at an awkward age and didn't have strong social skills. Concerned about his prospects for fitting in after their relocation, Eric had a heart-to-heart with his son. He asked about the activities Jayden enjoyed, and whether there was anything new he'd like to try. Surprisingly, Jayden said he'd always been interested in wrestling.

Jayden's interest turned out to be a budding talent, and when he joined the wrestling team at the new school, it became a lifelong passion. He tapped into his strength and confidence, and made friends that would stay with him for life.

No Kids? No Problem.

Not everyone reading this book will have small people running around. Whether you're a parent, an empty nester, a confirmed bachelor, or somewhere in between, it's important to seek out people you can relate to. Here are just a few of our favorite ways to meet other adults in town—even the ones who are as busy as you are.

Meetup groups and activities

Love it or hate it, in the age of the Internet, no man is an island. Even if you're not feeling like getting out of the house today, maybe you will next week—and we can practically guarantee that there'll be an activity-based group you can join when the time is right.

Do you like mountain biking? Discussing books? Wine tasting? Depending on the size of your town, there's likely to be a group meeting for at least one of the activities you enjoy. Finding these groups is relatively easy, thanks to sites like Meetup.com, local events calendars, and even posts on message boards, Craigslist, and so on.

Take the time to look up groups and activities that interest you, and sign yourself up. Having a scheduled activity makes it much easier to get yourself out of the house—and we've found that, even for more reserved people, activity-oriented groups tend to be very welcoming and easy to join. Plus, you stand a good chance of having some real fun with people who have similar interests.

Volunteering

Volunteering is an excellent way to meet people while using your skills (or picking up new ones) and accomplishing something you can be proud of. There are opportunities to volunteer everywhere: local and national charities, churches, arts programs, mentorships, parks, and schools. These types of organizations commonly rely on support from the community—support that goes beyond simply writing a check.

In particular, if you've recently retired, volunteering can be a highly fulfilling "new job" that, in addition to a more relaxed schedule, will let you offer your skills and experience to a cause you believe in. It's impossible *not* to make a few new connections in the process, and you can expect that the people working alongside you are likely to have some of the same priorities and values you do.

Spiritual or community gatherings

Not everyone attends religious services, but there are many cultural and community groups you might be interested in joining: from political gatherings, to ethnically oriented groups, to service organizations. Seek out the groups where you feel you might fit in or be welcomed.

Groups like this are some of the easiest to join, because they are usually set up to welcome new members—many of them will even have appointed "greeters" who seek out new people and show them the ropes. Even if you're only a bit curious, take the chance to discover what these groups offer. If it isn't for you, you can move on; but you might find yourself enveloped in an active community with very little effort or risk.

Lessons, lectures, and classes

What's something you've always wanted to learn? Now is the time to indulge your curiosity. Nearly every community has some (and often many) opportunities for learning: art history talks at the museum, cooking classes with local chefs, extended education programs through a college or university, etc. Picking up a new skill is the perfect way to fill some hours, meet new people, and put something on the calendar that you'll really look forward to.

Alumni and professional groups

Younger professionals and job seekers in particular can benefit from alumni gatherings and networking opportunities. Whether you want to meet people with similar experiences or similar ambitions, these slightly more formal gatherings can help you put your best foot forward in a new area.

Parties and outings

Don't deny the power of a good cocktail hour! If you're the type who enjoys conversation, consider hosting a party or inviting neighbors or colleagues out for a dinner or event. You or your partner might pick out a couple of new coworkers and ask them to bring their spouses or dates; or you could ask the parents of one of your kids' new friends to join you for a baseball game. Or just keep it casual, and ask a few coworkers what they're doing for Friday happy hour. No matter how busy people may seem when you catch them in the middle of work or errands, they will normally appreciate an excuse to relax, kick back, and get to know somebody new.

Online groups

Even if you're busy, you can usually find a few minutes to get online. Meetup.com is a great place to start, but there are other options to help you make connections locally. Try searching Facebook and other social networking sites, using the name of your new community as a search term. You may find neighborhood groups, networking groups, parent groups, and much more. We also recommend signing up for Nextdoor.com to connect with your immediate neighborhood. Even a basic message board is worth a shot; make some posts, introduce yourself, and see who responds.

Instant connection

Jenny had never really visited Boston before she moved there, and she had no idea what to expect. During her research, she found a Meetup group for moms, and posted, "I'm new here, can you give me your advice for how to get around?"

Within minutes, Jenny got a reply from another young mother who was new to the area. The two made plans to get out and explore the city together, which turned into a weekly date. They tried out reading programs at the libraries; visited museums; went to out-of-the-way sites; and in the process, became best friends.

When Fitting In is Tough

Let's face it: most of us aren't as dapper or charming as we'd like to be. Many of us are busy, stressed, or anxious about meeting new people. And sometimes, despite being dapper, charming, and ready to make friends—it doesn't happen right away.

If you're struggling to find people you can authentically connect with, know that great friendships don't always (or even usually) materialize quickly. Keep putting yourself out there, and keep trying new social circles until you find one you feel comfortable in.

Your attitude about making friends can actually be a bit of a self-fulfilling prophecy: if you trust that you will eventually meet and connect with some fantastic people, you'll be more enthusiastic about the process of finding them. It can be tough to convince yourself of this after a few strikeouts; we often hear, "I just don't think I understand people here." But trust us, there are wonderful people everywhere, in every town and every country.

If you're starting to feel defeated—or in the case of kids, if they're having significant problems that are affecting their performance and enthusiasm at school—don't be shy about seeking out someone to talk to. This could be a friend from back home, a spiritual advisor, or yes, a therapist or counselor. When we're feeling alone and misunderstood, it truly does help to find someone who's willing to listen and validate our experience. You've gone through a major life transition, and it's normal and natural to need a little extra support, especially when you don't have buddies nearby.

Finally, make the effort to keep your closest friendships alive, even from hundreds of miles away. It's easy to hop online and chat with most of the people who filled your life previously, but don't rely on superficial comments and "likes" to serve all of your emotional needs. Take the time to call or video chat with people who are really important to you. Many people set up weekly or even monthly chat dates with family and friends. A little reminder that you're loved and appreciated can go a long way.

Asking for help

Luke and his two kids relocated not long after his divorce, and he worried about their ability to cope with all the change, not to mention being geographically separated from their mother. Knowing they might need extra support, he sought out a family counselor and the three started sessions.

At first it was deeply uncomfortable, and the sessions were often awkward; but the family learned to communicate and to address the things that were weighing them down. Luke was able to better understand what his teenage children needed, and the family built trust that carried them through high school, college—and two more relocations.

Shellye's Tip: There are good people everywhere.

As I mentioned earlier, the very first time we moved, I told my husband, "I don't want to be living out of boxes forever. Let's give ourselves a deadline to be unpacked and settled in." To make that deadline stick, we made a slightly crazy decision: after six weeks in our new house, we were throwing a party. For what friends, you might ask? Well, we invited everybody we spoke to. Neighbors, even a handyman who did some repairs. And sure enough, after six weeks we were settled in enough to have our party.

We are both community people. We like to know our neighbors. I have my tricks for making that happen. For example, right after you move, it's very believable that you can't find a wrench, or a screwdriver, or a flashlight. So I knock on a neighbor's door and ask to borrow one. Now I've introduced myself, and then we talk again when I come back with the item, and maybe later I'll drop by with some cookies to thank them for the "lifesaver." Sometimes you have to create an excuse to meet people!

It can be harder for the kids to fit in at a new school. I remember when my daughter came home after a few weeks in a new place, and told me she didn't like anybody at her school. "They are all so superficial and fake," she told me.

"Listen," I said, "they are not all anything. What you're seeing are the people who want you to notice them. I guarantee that there are all kinds of people at your school, including people who share your values. But because they don't have such big personalities, you just haven't found them

yet." It did take a little while, but she got to be so attached to that school that eventually she didn't want to leave.

There are good people everywhere, but sometimes you need to go looking for them!

Smart Moves

Take Initiative.

You'll probably have to start conversations yourself, but you've got an easy icebreaker: "I'm new here." Find excuses to talk to people, and don't be afraid to ask for help or favors. This is your new community; give folks a chance to welcome you.

Get Involved.

Join groups, associations, and classes. You may not stick with them, but in our experience, an interest-oriented group is the ideal situation for meeting new people without much pressure or obligation. It works for shy people, too!

Activity: Social Goal Setting

Are you finding it hard to make socialization a priority? Maybe some people in your household are making friends, while others aren't sure how to meet new people? Or perhaps you're simply better when you have a to-do list. This activity is for you!

Make a copy of this sheet for each member of your household, and fill them out together. Make sure to give each other positive feedback and encouragement; meeting new people can make anyone feel vulnerable!

Things I'd Like to Try

Read this chapter and research activities, groups, or other opportunities that sound interesting. Keep a running list here:

_____

_____

_____

_____

_____

_____

_____

Now turn those ideas into goals: add the above activities to your calendar, or check them off your list one by one. Aim to get out and try one thing each week—for each family member!

Resource: Meetup Guide

Meetup.com is a highly user-friendly site, but there are still a few things to be aware of. Since we want everyone reading this book to get the most out of Meetup, we're sharing our top tips with you.

Sign up

It's difficult to browse Meetup without creating an account. Take the time to follow the registration process and add a few details about yourself.

Join lots of groups

Once you're signed up, you can use Meetup's search function to find groups in your area. Browse the full list and join absolutely every group that sounds like it could be fun. Why join them all? Because, once you've joined, you'll get emails about upcoming events—including relevant details like how many people will be attending, etc. This can keep you interested in the group, and help you decide which groups are most active and likely to be a match for you.

RSVP to (and attend) some events!

The hardest part of the process is actually getting yourself there—but make it a priority to follow through, and you'll reap the rewards. Once you're at an event, it should be relatively easy to strike up conversations. Don't forget your three magic words: "I'm new here."

Ask for contact information

If you connect with someone at a meeting, never assume they'll be back again for future events—ask for their email address or phone number right away. Whether or not they end up being your new best friend, remember that they joined a Meetup group for the same reason you did: to meet people.

Use the message boards

Message boards are optional on Meetup, so not all of your groups will include them. If one or more of your groups does have a board available, make a post introducing yourself; you can also use the boards to follow up and keep in touch with people between events.

Don't give up

If your first couple of events aren't great—if, for example, there aren't many people you can connect with, or the event isn't well managed—try, try again. Not every group will be a perfect match, and some groups or events will surprise you by being much more fun than you expect. It all comes down to how well the Meetup is organized, and who happens to be available on that date. If you keep at it, you're likely to find a group or event that's truly fun.

8. Job Hunting

Finding work that works for you

When Maria moved to Michigan in the 1990s, she found her job literally by accident: she slipped on ice and broke her leg. Stuck in bed recuperating, she was flipping through the paper and, out of curiosity, scanned the Help Wanted section. There it was: a job she was eminently qualified for. "Well," she thought, "why not check it out?"

Maria asked around to see if the company was reputable, prepared an application, and by the time her leg healed, she had a new job.

After years with the same employer, however, Maria found herself uprooted: her husband had been transferred, relocating the family to North Carolina. Suddenly, Maria was in a brand new community—and a brand new market. The industry she had worked in didn't even exist in the Southern Atlantic. And in today's job market, scanning classified ads was no longer a viable way to find a position. So Maria went to work at finding work—with lots of help from her coach at IMPACT Group.

It took several months, and many interviews, before Maria found a job she was excited about, with good pay and a company culture she enjoyed. Was it worth the wait? A job you love is always worth searching for, and after spending years at a job that had made her truly happy, Maria knew she'd never settle for anything less.

This chapter will update you with the strategies Maria, and most modern job seekers, use to stay competitive, weigh opportunities, and stand out in crowded pools of applicants. If you've been out of the job market for a while, we'll catch you up with technology and practices. And if you're feeling a little fear about the prospect of a months-long job hunt, we'll load you up with all the tools you need to make it go smoothly.

One caveat: When you're serious about your job hunt, it's always a good idea to get some help. There's no such thing as a professional job seeker; it's a learning process for everyone. This chapter is by no means a comprehensive job search resource. Don't be afraid to admit what you don't know, and ask a career coach or another hiring professional to give you guidance. In our experience, this can cut your job search time in half!

A hand up

Fresh out of college, Jay's first job turned out to be a nightmare. He found himself back on the market, in a new city with a threadbare resume. In the first month, Jay sent out at least a hundred applications, but his field was competitive, and with no experience, he got no responses.

Frustrated, Jay turned to an online alumni group to ask for advice. In addition to receiving good tips, he found himself invited to a baseball game with a group of graduates of all ages. A fellow alumnus introduced Jay to his wife—who was hiring young, hungry salespeople. Jay took the chance, and within ten years, had risen to VP with the same company.

Targeting Your Search

There sure are a lot of jobs available—so why is it such a challenge to find one you want? The job search, for most people, starts with online job boards that may have hundreds, even thousands, of listings in your area.

After the first few moments of overwhelm, it usually becomes clear that a more directed search is needed. How will you sift through all the posted jobs to find the ones with true potential?

At the end of this chapter, you'll find a job search worksheet that will help you clarify your priorities. It's important to define your dream job, so you can find it (or something like it) among all the possibilities. As always, having crystal-clear priorities will help you cut through any confusion and stay on track to find the job you really want. We recommend you take the time to create your personal elevator pitch, so you can be ready to tell people the kind of job you are looking for and what *you* can bring to *them*.

Once you understand what you're looking for, it's time to get smart about your search. Don't just keep scanning the same job boards! Our experts never recommend looking for a job simply by checking out job aggregator boards and applying to a listed position completely cold. If this is your only strategy, you can expect your job hunt to take much, much longer than you want it to.

Thanks to those same job boards you're currently surfing, employers can be flooded with hundreds of applications for a single position—far too many to review carefully, let alone follow up or interview. In a crowded pool of applicants, even if you're qualified for the job, you'll be lucky to get noticed.

Instead, take a targeted approach. Begin by researching the companies in your area and field, and search their websites for any openings. Use your dream job profile, and start networking your way toward it (more on that to follow). Let job boards be your backup plan, and focus your energy on creating the connections that will lead you toward that perfect career.

Networking: It's Not Optional

Hypothetical: You're a hiring manager, and you have one hundred applications to review. Only one of them was sent to you by a trusted colleague;

the rest came in over the Internet. Which application are you going to look at first?

The true key to landing that dream job is to do it the old-fashioned way. Even in this connected age, one-on-one interactions are still the best method to get someone's attention. In other words: it's all about who you know.

If you've done some networking before, now is the time to jump back into the fray. If you're new to the experience, there are a few ways to make it easier and more effective. Here are some of our experts' top tips:

Get to Know LinkedIn

As an active job seeker, you need an up-to-date, active LinkedIn profile. But don't stop there. This site is bursting with opportunities to connect with colleagues and yes, even jobs. As you meet people at your kids' school, around town, and at your partner's company, begin to connect with them, which will help grow your LinkedIn network in the new community.

Join groups related to your field, your location, and your background. Professional associations, local networking groups, alumni groups, and so on are all easy entry points to career conversations. When you join a group, introduce yourself and let people know what you're looking for: "I just moved to Houston and am seeking a cause-oriented organization in need of a talented marketing manager!"

LinkedIn is also the place to further your dream-job targeting campaign: look up your desired employer, see who works there, and strategize to connect with them. We don't recommend you be pushy, but asking a few questions about the company can be a good way to get to know a potential employer. This is particularly effective if they're *not* hiring: managers will be more willing to talk if they're not flooded with applicants. Use this informal, informational connection to find out what you can offer the company in the future.

Finally, LinkedIn job boards tend to be a better place to do your hunting; while this mostly applies to mid-level employees and up, anyone can view job listings. One of the major benefits to viewing jobs on LinkedIn is the ability to use any potential connections to get you an introduction and reference. Create email alerts to let you know when jobs that fit your profile are added.

Network Everywhere

Some of your most effective connections might be the unexpected ones. Start with your real estate agent, your banker, your insurance broker… these service providers work with you, as well as a large number of professionals in your area. If you're doing business with someone, you've got a professional relationship—and service providers like these tend to have robust networks, because their businesses depend on them. They are great ones to connect with on LinkedIn!

Our #1 networking tip: tell everybody you're looking for a job. From the mailman, to your neighbor, to your mortgage lender, make sure everyone knows you're looking. Always be prepared to explain what type of job you want, and what you have to offer. You never know what connections will arise from a little small talk!

Formal Networking

Networking groups aren't just a good place to land a job; they're also wonderful opportunities to make a few friends. Make a point of attending at least a couple of events per month, and use those three magic words—"I'm new here"—to break the ice.

Networking goes both ways! When networking, and particularly at formal gatherings, remember to listen as much as you speak. Find out not just what other people can do for you, but what you might be able to do for them. At times, it can take a few conversations before you really click on a mutually beneficial solution—but they happen more often than you might expect.

Finally, always go a few steps further to keep your new connections alive. We're all busy; even a wonderful conversation can turn into an afterthought after the meeting is over and life crashes back in. Take the time to send follow-up emails, connect on LinkedIn, make phone calls, or even send a handwritten note to let your new contacts know that you appreciate their time. Those little gestures can make all the difference when it's time to follow up on a job lead!

It's who you know

Ray, an experienced executive, got a LinkedIn connection request from his new neighbor, and when she knocked on his door the next day, he was certain she would ask him for a job—but instead, she asked him for an introduction to one of his contacts. "You seem to know everybody in town," Amy said. "Could you help me get noticed? I really want this job."

Having shared a fence with Amy and her husband for a few months, Ray thought he could recommend her character, if not her work. He agreed to hand her resume to his colleague.

Job Applications

In the modern job market, you can expect to fill out most of your applications using online forms. This process can take some time, and it tends to quash creativity a bit—which is the point. When applying for jobs online, always follow instructions to the letter. In many cases, applications that don't comply will simply be thrown out.

Your one chance to shine is through a powerful cover letter. Always tailor your letter to the job, explaining why you want to work there and how you can contribute to this specific organization. Take the opportunity here to let your personality and accomplishments shine through.

One of the toughest parts of this process is that many employers will instruct applicants not to follow up via phone or email. If this is the case, resist the urge to call and check on your application! However, if no such note exists, then we do recommend you give it a shot.

Interviewing

When you finally get the call for an interview, it's time to go into study mode. Particularly if you're on an ambitious career track, nailing the interview is a challenge worth preparing for. **Even if you haven't worked with a career or job coach before, this is the moment where a qualified expert can really be of help to you. At the very least, ask a friend or colleague to help you prepare.**

Many people enjoy conducting mock interviews, but this isn't necessary for everyone. A good plan is to research common interview questions, prepare your answers, and practice them many times over until they feel natural. You might keep a list in your phone, and go over it while you're waiting in line. Whatever your preferred study method, keep up with it so when you arrive for the interview, you're collected and prepared.

We can't teach you everything we know about interviewing in this chapter (that's another book on its own!), but we will remind you of one very important thing to keep in mind: an interview isn't just for the employer to get to know you; it's also your opportunity to get to know them.

Asking questions during the interview can also help you connect with the interviewer. Find out how long he or she has worked for the company, and whether they're from the area originally. Ask about the best parts of working for this organization. In particular, pose questions related to your own job priorities.

Once the interview is over, follow-up is absolutely required. Never let your potential employer doubt your interest in the job. Follow up politely, and if you don't connect with the hiring manager, offer a time that you can call back. When you call back at that time, you just might be able to talk to them; if not, your continued interest will be noted!

Know your stuff

Lynne was choosy about the jobs she applied for, so when one of them called her for an interview, she was fully prepared. Not only had she been practicing her interview questions, but she had researched the company's product line and even come up with some ideas.

One of the first interview questions was, "Are you familiar with our products?" Lynne launched into her response with full detail. Later, she was surprised to learn that some other applicants had not done their research—and that question had ended their interviews on the spot. Thanks to her preparation, Lynne succeeded, and started work two weeks later.

How Do You Come Across?

It goes without saying that, throughout this process, you should be unfailingly polite and professional. However, if you haven't spent a lot of time in the professional world—or if it's been a long time since you've inter-viewed—you may not be fully aware of how others perceive you.

Don't be shy; ask for advice! Ask friends and colleagues, as well as experts. Career coaches, speaking coaches, even style coaches are always available for consultations on everything from your haircut to your interview man-ner. Again, there's no such thing as a professional job seeker, but there are many professionals who can aid your job search. Make use of their services to make your search easier!

Shellye's Tip: Help employers find you

These days, so many jobs—especially the more senior roles—are filled through the network of people you know. If you don't have that network in the new area, start to build it immediately.

If you're in a specific profession (accountant, architect, and so on), there is almost always going to be a professional as-sociation in your area. Go to those meetings. Get involved. Let people know about yourself, and that you're looking. These are the people who are most likely to know about opportunities in your field!

In these days of social media, you certainly need to be on LinkedIn. Set up or update your profile, and if you have an area of expertise, start writing about it. At my company, we use social media to find people with specific skills and ex-perience. If you are posting about the topics we're looking at, we will look at you.

Create an environment in which you can be found by em-ployers!

Smart Moves

Network, Network, Network!

Every person you meet is a possible professional contact or resource. It truly is all about who you know, so get out and meet as many people as you can. Don't forget to prepare your elevator pitch to quickly tell people who you are and what you're looking for.

Prepare Now, Relax Later.

Preparing for interviews is crucial, not just so you come across professionally, but so you can feel relaxed and confident when it matters. Eventually, you will have an interview for the job you really want—will you be ready to nail it?

Worksheet: Designing Your Dream Job

Know what you want, and you're much more likely to find it! Use this worksheet to lay out your expectations. Be honest about what you really want, and clear about your top priorities.

What are some positions or career paths you would like to explore?

_____

_____

_____

_____

_____

What are your strongest skills and interests? What do you excel at?

_____

_____

_____

_____

_____

Where would you like to be professionally in five years?

_____

_____

_____

_____

_____

What is your desired salary?

_____

What's the smallest salary you will accept?

_____

When do you need to start working to avoid financial difficulty?

- Within the next three months

- Within the next six months

- More than six months from now

What types of benefits do you expect to receive?

Rank the following options from 1 (absolutely necessary) to 5 (not needed).

_____ Health insurance for me

_____ Health insurance for my family

_____ 401(k) or retirement package

_____ Two weeks or more of vacation time annually

_____ Ability to accumulate vacation and/or sick time

_____ Profit sharing or stock options

_____ Tuition reimbursement

_____ Wellness programs

_____ Flexible hours or telecommuting

_____ Childcare, elder care, or dependent care

_____ Transportation reimbursement

_____ Employee assistance programs

How much time are you willing to spend commuting, each way?

☐ Up to twenty minutes

☐ Up to forty minutes

☐ Up to an hour

☐ Over an hour

What type of company culture are you interested in?

Thinking about the work environment you'd most enjoy, circle any of the descriptors that appeal to you.

Open floor plan / Private offices

Startup / Established

Large corporation / Small business

Flexible hours / Clear schedule expectations

Flat organizational structure / Frequent opportunities for advancement

Cause-oriented / Profit-oriented

Add your own ideas below:

Worksheet: Job Application Tracker

As you apply for jobs, it's easy to lose track of the details. Keep a log of each job you apply to, to help you track your progress and stay current with potential opportunities.

Download this worksheet at www.ThisSideUpGuide.com.

Job Title	Company	Hiring Mgr.	Phone/Email	Date Applied	Status/Notes

9. Settling In

Embarking on your next chapter in life

By the time you read this chapter, the dust may have settled (even if it's settling on a few still-packed boxes). Perhaps you've got the kids off to school or the morning commute figured out. Your to-do list is mostly checked off.

Now what?

After the first few weeks in your new place, it's no longer exactly new—but it isn't exactly "home" yet either. Now is the moment to decide what you want your new life to *really* look like, and how you want to live in it. The possibilities are, if not endless, extremely numerous. And finally, you've got a little time to explore them!

Nothing will happen overnight. If you're still learning the ropes at a new job or figuring out where the grocery stores are (or both), you may not have much time to settle in or get involved in your community. Even though you're busy now, eventually you'll have some Saturdays free. How would you like to fill them? Start sowing the seeds now, and you'll reap the benefits soon enough.

The dream house

Jim and Sharon were finally moving back to the South, and Sharon was ready to pursue her lifelong dream of owning, and rehabilitating, a Victorian house. They bought a fixer-upper in a neighborhood that had once been thriving, and showed signs of coming back to life. In fact, the house they bought had been abandoned for years, and was considered a local blight.

Soon after they took possession, the renovations began. Sharon was retired, so she made it her job—and within days, she had her first visitor. Before long, neighbor after neighbor was stopping by to see the progress and thank her for bringing back the beauty of this lovely old home. She soon made friends throughout town and even in the city building department while she found her own fulfillment in following through on a life goal.

Home Sweet (Happy, Healthy) Home

Now that you've got a few moments to breathe, it's a good time to think about the things that made you happy and healthy pre-relocation, and find ways to pursue them again. For many people, this will be an easy decision: if you're a golfer or a snowboarder, odds are strong that you've already looked up the best courses or slopes in your area. Give yourself the time to follow through on that research. Make a few hours in your week to try out your favorite activities. Yes, that's right—you're allowed to just go have some fun.

Another top priority for many people, especially those with kids, is finding good healthcare providers. While the prospect of researching doctors may not be particularly thrilling, this is a good opportunity to ask your neighbors for recommendations. Referrals make all the difference in finding the best doctors in town. Approach your neighbors in person, or use online groups or services like Nextdoor.com to pose your question to a wider audience. With any luck, you'll also make a few friends.

A new beginning

Kelly had spent decades raising a family, but once the kids had left home, she and her husband decided to divorce. She found a job in Denver, and moved into her own place for the first time since college.

Right away, Kelly knew she wanted to get out, join the dating world, and meet some new people to go with her brand-new life. As soon as she unpacked, she joined the gym and a local hiking group, and set up an online dating profile. Within weeks, Kelly had gone on a few dates and was learning her way around town, in the company of new friends.

The Crossroads

Here at the threshold of your new home and life, you have a big opportunity that many people aren't lucky enough to experience: you have a chance at a fresh start (or something close to it). Is there anything you've always wanted to try? Something you want to change? Now is the moment to take the first steps in a new direction.

Again, in the first weeks while you're unpacking and getting settled, you may not have much time to take up swing dancing classes. Nonetheless, you probably have time to find out when and where they're held, and even sign up for one next month.

One of the keys to making ideas become realities is to start taking action before you're totally ready. That includes signing up for activities and groups, as well as making the time to explore, have fun, and try all those new things you're excited about. In other words: don't let long work hours and endless chores become excuses that get in the way of following a dream or two! Before you know it, you'll be establishing routines in the new location, so be intentional about starting the right ones.

This is the time to revisit those priorities you set all the way back at the start of this process. Hopefully, you've had them in mind throughout, and have allowed them to guide some of your decisions. With any luck, you were able to move into a community that has some of the services and opportunities you were looking for. Now ask yourself—how am I acting on those ideas in my daily life?

Community in unexpected places

Jared and his family were truly sorry to leave Utah. As a young Mormon family, they had enjoyed the community support and the feeling of belonging—but Jared's company had folded, and he found work in California.

For the first few days, everything was focused on getting the family settled in a new, and smaller, house. But then they visited the local church for the first time, and found they had unknowingly moved to a community with a high Mormon population. Somehow, in their research, they hadn't uncovered this fact; the discovery completely turned their experiences around, and they felt at home in a way they had not expected.

What's Holding You Back?

Motivation is a big part of making the settling-in process a success, but motivation alone doesn't clear your calendar, and life tends to get in the way of all our awesome ambitions. If things aren't unfolding exactly as you planned—surprise! You're normal.

Truly, the best advice we can offer you at this point is not to compare your experience to others' lives, or even to your own ideas of how it should be going. Instead, take stock of your options and do what's best for you.

For example, many younger professionals find themselves working much longer hours, and being more worn out after work and commute, than they expected. The at-home parent might find that the to-do list never seems to get any shorter, while their partner is working too much and can't help with the house and kids. Things rarely work out as planned, for anyone!

Whatever roadblocks appear in your path, there's always a way over (or around) them. Rather than beating yourself up for not making friends yet, why not try introducing yourself to coworkers and organizing a Friday happy hour? Or, take a break from your ambitious redecorating plans for a few weeks and give yourself time to finally take that pottery class? Why not ask the neighbors for babysitter recommendations, leave the kids at home, and go on a walking tour of the town some night this week?

If none of that is possible, have no fear—it will be, soon enough. Keep planning for the future you want, and keep a positive outlook!

Going back home

When she moved to London, Vanessa knew she wouldn't feel at home right away, and sure enough, it took about two years to really settle in. When she met others who had moved recently, she assured them: "It takes two years, but it will happen for you too."

Still, when her job in London was finished, Vanessa assumed she'd be able to easily readjust to life in the city she'd grown up in. She was bowled over to discover that the homecoming wasn't nearly as seamless as she expected: despite knowing her way around town and having friends and family nearby, Vanessa still had to find a new school for her son, doctors, stores—and a job. In the end, it took another year before things stabilized—but they did!

Kids and Fitting In

Sometimes, at this stage, kids struggle to find their spot in the social order. This can be most acute for middle schoolers, but it happens to everyone now and then; fitting in at a new school and community is tough.

As a parent with your children's best interest in mind, you know what they need better than anyone. How can you help them get it? Just like you, your kids are at their own crossroads. Ask them what they might like to try or change, and they may surprise you with their answers.

In particular, signing up for new activities can help kids have something to get excited about. In the case of middle schoolers, they may have emerging talents or interests in sports, music, science, art, or theater that can become lifelong passions. It's worthwhile to try a few things to see what clicks—with the clear understanding that they don't have to succeed in every hobby.

There's also plenty to be said for good old-fashioned family time—a luxury in today's world, but a luxury any family can afford. Sometimes, what we really need is just to spend time around the people who know us well, and with whom we can let our guard down for a few minutes.

Remember to visit RelocatingKids.com for good advice and ideas for parents and kids alike. You're not alone in this, and help is available!

Final Word: It Takes Time

No matter how excited (or how anxious) you are about the possibilities that lie before you; no matter how outgoing and friendly you are; no matter how willing you are to take life by the horns…building a new life takes longer than you expect.

Instead of focusing on how quickly or how slowly you're settling in, put your energy into crafting a well-designed life that truly suits you. Make the effort to discover all the possibilities; invest energy into your family, friendships, and activities; and carefully select the things that will help you achieve your goals. Time has a way of flowing past no matter what we do, but if you focus on creating meaningful experiences, those experiences will be your rewards.

Shellye's Tip: Create your community on your terms

When we moved to California, I wanted to meet people and get involved. But I knew that, as a CEO, my time would be limited. Groups that met at specific times might be difficult for me. So I decided, I like to cook, I like to entertain, why not start a gourmet dinner club?

Everywhere we went, every person we met, I'd offhandedly ask, "Oh, by the way, do you happen to like to cook?" I didn't care if they were good at it, I just wanted to know if they liked cooking. I asked everyone: a woman I met at the gym, some friends a cousin had introduced us to, people I met at parties. We relocated in August, and hosted the first dinner party the following spring. It started as a group of ten people or so, and thirteen years later we're going strong with fifty members!

Getting engaged in your community is what makes a place feel like home. Find something you are excited to do, and get involved.

Smart Moves

Don't Compare.

Everyone's experience will be different, even within your own family. Nobody can tell you what you're "supposed" to be feeling, except you. When we're feeling vulnerable or lonely, it's easy to think we're the only ones having trouble—but it really is a challenge for everyone, in different ways and at different times.

Stay Positive.

Remember your promise to keep a positive attitude. Look for the bright side, even if it's hidden behind a cloud, and eventually you will find the things that make you happy and excited to be starting this new adventure.

Worksheet: Gotta vs. Wanna

This one is pretty straightforward. When you've got lots of tasks on your to-do list, it's important to prioritize. Use this worksheet to help you find time for the things you're excited about, instead of being swept away by responsibilities!

Step 1: List everything on your to-do list.

Sort everything into two categories: the "gottas" or things you absolutely have to do, and the "wannas" or things you want to do if you can make the time. For example, work is a "gotta," while going roller skating is a "wanna."

GOTTA   WANNA

_____   _____

_____   _____

_____   _____

_____   _____

_____   _____

_____   _____

_____   _____

_____   _____

_____   _____

Step 2: Re-prioritize.

Now, go back through the "gottas" and move as many of them as you can to the opposite column. For example, finding a gardener—unless it's required by your homeowner's association, that's not a dire necessity.

The goal here is to lower the priority of some of the things you feel you have to do, so you can make time for the things that will make your life more fun and interesting.

Step 3: Revisit your priorities.

Go back to the priorities you established in Chapter One. Write them here, along with any ideas for how you can follow through on them in your daily or weekly activities.

_____

_____

_____

_____

_____

_____

_____

_____

Worksheet: Kids' Dreambook

Old enough to make your own choices about how to spend your time outside of school? This worksheet can help you get new ideas for things to try.

If you didn't have to go to school at all, what would you do instead?

_____

_____

_____

_____

_____

Do you spend more time listening to music, looking at (or making) art, playing games, or moving around? Why?

_____

_____

_____

_____

_____

What's something you've seen another person do that you want to try?

_____

_____

_____

_____

_____

If you could take lessons to learn anything (even something imaginary), what would you want to learn?

_____

_____

_____

_____

_____

Exercise: Daily Gratitude

Optimism and gratitude aren't personality traits—they're habits, and habits that can really help improve your mood and outlook. It's no secret that some of the happiest people on Earth are masters at looking on the bright side, no matter what's happening.

Keep your own spirits high by practicing a little gratitude. It only takes a few minutes a day, but it can change your mind on a deep level.

For this exercise, simply jot down three things you're grateful for. That's it! One day, you might be grateful for your home, your family, and your job. The next day, it might be a nice thing somebody said to you, that donut you ate for breakfast, and a new pair of shoes. On a tough day, you might just be grateful that it stopped raining, that you've got a friend you can talk to, and that your car started this morning. It doesn't matter what you write down; just keep writing down three things every day.

This can also be a wonderful family exercise when more than one person is having a difficult time. Sometimes when we're struggling, it helps to remind each other that we're in it together, that we are loved, and that there is always a silver lining. Start by writing down three things now:

1. _____

2. _____

3. _____

Exercise: Visualize Your Future

This creative exercise is good for the whole family, and will help you bring the future into focus. It's easier to know what to do today, if you know how it will affect you tomorrow!

Repeat this exercise whenever you're feeling uncertain about what you want or where you're headed.

What do I want to happen tomorrow?

_____

_____

_____

_____

_____

What do I want to happen next week?

_____

_____

_____

_____

_____

What do I want to happen in the next year?

_____

_____

_____

_____

_____

What do I want to happen in the next five years?

_____

_____

_____

_____

Now that you've answered the five-year question, have any of the other answers changed?

_____

_____

_____

_____

_____

Conclusion

New Life vs. Old Life: What will you create?

Congratulations! You've made it to the end of this book, and that means you've accomplished a lot. From the initial decision to move, through the emotional roller coaster of packing and planning, to finding a new home and getting everybody there in one piece (more or less). You likely have made new friends, conducted a job search, or managed school registrations and doctor's appointments. You've probably figured out the essentials of how your life works now. And you've undoubtedly overcome a few surprises!

This in no way means that your journey is over. **Depending on your experiences, your personality, your actions, and all those unpredictable things we call "life," your adjustment can take weeks, months, even years. Eventually, you will feel at home—but nobody can tell you how long it will take, or what "home" truly means to you.**

You're the same person, just in a different place. How can you move forward and embrace the future, while still remaining true to yourself? As always, the key is your own attitude. Stay confident in yourself, and choose to have a positive experience—and you will find a way!

Homesick? FOMO? Don't Let It Get You Down

Homesickness and FOMO (Fear Of Missing Out) can run rampant if you've left a tight-knit group of friends. Hearing about their good times or seeing photos online, it can really hurt to see that their lives have gone on without you. But here's the thing: your life has gone on, too.

Even the closest relationships ebb and flow, and new people move in and out of our lives. **Remember that your next best friend is out there waiting to meet you and create a whole new set of memories. Though it can be tempting to fixate on the people and experiences we miss—and though it's healthy to keep those memories close—clinging to the past is a sure-fire way to miss out on the future.**

So stop refreshing all those photos of your old buddies at happy hour, and go out to your own happy hour event! Open yourself up to the possibility of new experiences and new friends, and they will come to you.

That said, your old friends can still be a powerful source of support and motivation. If you're feeling down, why not let them know and ask for a little positive reinforcement? The people who care about you—aside from missing you as much as you miss them—probably wish you the best and will be happy to tell you so. Ask for support when you need it.

It's a Marathon...

...not a sprint. Big life changes always take longer than we expect, and certainly longer than we really want; your best bet is to learn to enjoy the process of change. Don't push yourself outside your comfort zone *every* day, but go at your own speed. Avoid comparing: if your spouse, your son, or anybody else seems to be settling in like a duck to water, that's wonderful—but it doesn't say anything about your own experience. There's really no rule for how long these things "should" take. What matters is how happy you are.

How far into the future can *you* see? Most of us can't see as far as next Tuesday, let alone next month or next year. You really don't know what will happen next, but you can set goals and work toward achieving them. Want to make a new friend? You may not be able to control when or how it will happen, but if you put in the effort, you will undoubtedly connect with somebody. Want to start a new career? It's a matter of getting the training, experience, and connections you need. Want to feel at home in a new city? You know how to do it, and now it's just a matter of time and effort.

Relocation is one of the most exciting, upending, world-shaking experiences any of us goes through. Whether you're doing this for the first time or the twentieth, there will always be new experiences, new challenges, new opportunities, and new people. The one thing that never changes is *you*.

Keep on being you, no matter where you are, and it'll start to feel like home—and always remember to keep your right side up. We believe in you!

Acknowledgements

Partners in crime during the writing of this book: particularly Debbie Hilke for sharing the vision and Jessica Reeder for helping me get the words out. Big thanks to Shellye Archambeau for your invaluable insights and additions to the book. Also Kristy Fairbanks and Melanie Winograd for their feedback along the way, and Paige Craven, for keeping us on track. Ed Chaffin and Max Barnett have been hugely critical in moving our business forward while I have been involved in the writing of this book, and thank you to Brook Goskowski and Ed Marshall for your passion for the work we do in helping relocating families.

Thank you to the entire team at IMPACT Group for sharing your experiences to help pull this book together. Thanks especially to Tanya Fite for your help in lining up all the interviews, Linda Ryan for your passion, Christina Callahan for your heart, and our consultants who played such a pivotal role: Shelby McGuire Canlas, Vicki Prasch, Kathleen Johnson, Sue Ellison, Heather Eller, Laura Todt-Stockman, Sue Wegrzyn, Sally Sinclair, Jim Wojtak, Carrie LeMahieu, Doug Hipp, Tracy Collins, Anita Cole, and Laura Davison. I couldn't have done it without you!

IMPACT Group clients who have believed in us over the years have also played a big part in us having the ability to write this book. Companies like Johnson & Johnson, Pfizer, Boeing, PepsiCo, Genentech, AT&T, and Amazon, truly care about their people and generously support their employees and their families during job-related moves.

I stood on the shoulders of giants as I wrote this book. Not only was I guided by IMPACT Group's expert coaches, but a special thanks to Mary

Quigg, founder of Vandover, and the memory of Sally White, founder of Sally White & Associates, whose companies have become part of the IMPACT Group family. I am blessed to be a part of the histories of these wonderful companies and these women's stories.

The greatest "giant" of all to me is my mother. I could have never written this book without the inspiration of my mother, Laura Herring. First of all, thank you for starting such an inspirational company, founded on the principles of making a positive difference in people's lives. Your vision and passion inspires me and so many others! I also owe you a huge debt of gratitude for trusting me with your "second child." Thank you for that trust and for giving me the opportunity to also make it my own, too. I would have never embarked on this book journey, though, had I not seen it first hand through the launch of your book, *No Fear Allowed*! I was so excited by the success of your book, that I felt called to write *This Side Up*! Thanks to my dad, Mike, for your never-ending support of both mom and me, and for keeping us from chasing after shiny objects. I love you both so much!

Finally, to Ted—thank you for joining me on the adventure of life. I love you and I can't wait for what's to come for you, Kennedy, and me.

Lauren

Additional Resources

Real Estate:

www.zillow.com

www.trulia.com

www.realtor.com

Online real estate research

Your Amazing Itty Bitty Sell Your Home Book: 15 Simple Steps on How to Stage and Sell Your Home - Fast!, by Eduardo Mendoza

Decluttering Your House:

The Life-Changing Magic of Tidying Up: The Japanese Art of Decluttering and Organizing, by Marie Kondo

Learning About the New Community:

www.neighborhoodscout.com

Using the "Match" feature on their homepage, enter in your current community and this site will refer you to the best match in your new area.

www.areavibes.com

This site has an easy to use interface to learn about and compare communities at a glance as well as in depth.

http://www.payscale.com/cost-of-living-calculator

Understand how far your money will go in the new community.

Getting Things Set Up:

www.usps.com

Forward mail using the US Post Office's website.

www.osconnects.com

OneSource Solutions is a free resource that can help connect most of the utilities for your new house.

www.angieslist.com or www.homeadvisor.com

Websites with recommended local contractors, handymen, lawn care, and more.

www.eac.gov

Find links to register to vote in your state.

Feeling Settled:

www.thissideupguide.com

Access all the worksheets and exercises from this book on our website!

www.relocatingkids.com

A website with games and resources for kids to get involved with and excited about the move.

www.newcomersclub.com

A global organization for the purpose of helping people connect in their new community.

www.meetup.com

Join groups by social activities and personal preferences to find likeminded people in your new area.

www.urbansitter.com or www.care.com

Resources for finding local babysitters and other child care help. These sites include recommendations and certifications for care givers to help newcomers feel more comfortable.

www.ratemds.com or www.healthgrades.com

Find doctors by specialty and location along with reviews from past patients.

Local libraries are also great resources for learning about the new community and upcoming events.

About Shellye Archambeau

Shellye Archambeau is a wife, mother, super-planner, and the CEO of MetricStream, a company focused on simplifying risk management and compliance to improve business performance. Under her leadership, MetricStream has grown into a global market leader recognized for growth and innovation.

Shellye serves on the Board of Directors of Verizon Communications, Inc. and Nordstrom, Inc. She has led initiatives and Washington, DC delegations to address regulatory compliance issues, and to improve governance.

Shellye also pens a column on leadership and entrepreneurship for Xconomy, and is frequently quoted in top tier media publications, including the *Wall Street Journal*, *New York Times*, *Compliance Week*, and *Silicon Valley Business Journal*. She is a much sought-after speaker who has presented on risk and compliance issues to Fortune 500 corporations, members of Congress, and various associations, including NASDAQ.

In April 2013, Shellye was named the "#2 Most Influential African American in Technology" by Business Insider.

About the Author

Lauren Herring passionately leads IMPACT Group as CEO, where she has transformed the company into a global leader in supporting employees and their families through personal and professional transitions. Lauren officially joined IMPACT Group in 2001 as an account manager; however, relocation has been in her blood ever since her mom, Laura, started the company back in 1988. She looks back fondly on her early days of collating relocation kits for families for a dime a piece. Over the years, these collated kits evolved into *This Side Up!*

During her time leading IMPACT Group, Lauren has acquired two other woman-owned companies focused on helping families successfully relocate globally. She has also added to the company's core competency of coaching to build a leadership development practice, and has taken the company global, with services currently available in over 60 countries.

Lauren has been awarded the prestigious Game Changer Award by *Workforce Magazine*, and Most Influential Women Award by the *St. Louis Business Journal*. She also received the Global HR Innovator of the Year Award, presented by *GlobalHR Magazine*. She is an internationally recognized speaker on the topic of career development and global mobility, has been quoted in the *Wall Street Journal* and *Forbes Magazine*, and has published in *HR Executive* and *GlobalHR Magazine*, among others. She is fluent in Spanish, and prior to joining IMPACT Group, Lauren worked in economic development in Puerto Rico.

Lauren holds a Master's in Business Administration from Washington University in St. Louis and a Bachelor's in Marketing from the University of

Notre Dame. Lauren is on the Board for the St. Louis Regional Chamber, where she is excited to support the economic development of the St. Louis community. She is also on the Board of the United Way of Greater St. Louis, COCA (the Center of Creative Arts), and Connections to Success, where she dedicates her expertise, resources and time to making a difference in her community and others' lives.

At the time of the launch of *This Side Up*, Lauren is embarking on the next phase of her life, and is thrilled to have Ted and Kennedy by her side from this point forward.